# #PaintTheWorld

## HOW TO CONNECT PEOPLE WITH YOUR TALENT

# COPYRIGHT DISCLAIMER

# REVIEWS FOR #WRITESTORM

*"A.L. Mengel does a fantastic job in not only explaining his methodology, but giving you the reader and prospective author the guidelines in how to use it in your own writing style/lifestyle."* —AUTHOR JEREMY CROSTON, Drakovia series, The Negative Man series.

*"Mengel has simplified and clarified the process, and made the idea of sitting and writing as easy as a sip of coffee (which we all need)."* — AUTHOR MICHAEL STERN, Quantum Touch series

*"This book completely revolutionized my writing! I cannot rave about it enough!"* — AUTHOR D.M. CAIN, The Light and Shadow Chronicles

# FOR MY FATHERS

# AND FOR TY

*Three brilliant business minds who have advised me over the years as I have taken forward steps on my creative journey. Thank you for opening my eyes – and my actions – to the business side of writing.*

# FROM THE AUTHOR

As I write this, the world has been in an era of uncertainty. It's June 2020, and this book soared into my life on wings. *#Writestorm* happened kind of the same way. But there's that old saying…good things take time. But great things happen all at once. And *#PaintTheWorld* just so happens to be one of those great things.

This book was written to be a money maker for you.

The fellow independently published authors, independently recorded artists, musicians and start-up entrepreneurs who don't have those deep pockets that the big corporations, publishers and record labels do, have unique challenges in the marketplace. But they can also be seen by the world.

We're all artists.

And we all must wear the different hats.

And sometimes those hats don't always fit quite right.

This book is about making those adjustments, so our visions can be seen by the world too.

Because we have to find a way to become the expert in almost everything pertaining to our craft or business venture, and also become an expert in marketing and promoting. So we have to find our way. It's a long path, with a lot of stepping stones, and we won't always hit the mark. But one thing is for certain – that this book will show you how I took steps, over years, to reach an audience of nearly a half million.

Not every step on the path was the right one. But all together, I've found that I've been headed in the right direction. This book aims to help you on your own promotional journey, as it has for me.

Now let's get started, and lets *#PaintTheWorld...*

- *A.L. Mengel*

# BOOKSHELF

## FROM THE TALES OF TARTARUS

*Ashes*

*The Quest for Immortality*

*The Blood Decanter*

*War Angel*

## FROM THE ASTRAL FILES

*The Mortician*

## FROM THE VEGA CHRONICLES

*The Wandering Star*

*The Europa Effect*

*The Arrival of Destiny*

*Battle of the Trinity*

## OTHER WORKS

*#Writestorm*

*The Other Side of the Door*

*Curtains and Fan Blades*

*#TheEraOf (Video Storytelling)*

*#TakeAJourney2018 (Book Tour)*

# TABLE OF CONTENTS

## THE FOUR "I" STATEMENTS

## THE FOUR "HOW" STATEMENTS

# PART ONE:

# THE "I" STATEMENTS

*Be a doer, not a dreamer. And by doing, one has the power to achieve their dreams.* - **#WRITESTORM**

# ONE

**I AM MY BRAND.**

AUTHORS, SINGERS, AND START-UP ENTREPRENEURS flood social media news feeds with the next best thing: the writers have written the best novel, the singers have an amazing not-to-be-missed album, and the entrepreneurs have a business model or product that no consumer can be without. While it is common for the mainstream A-listers to have their offerings on social media, they and their representatives have deep pockets, and the process in this book is not for those who do.

It's also quite necessary for the indies and start-ups to have their presence as well. The internet can make or break one who is just starting out. But the sea of social media promises can be daunting, overwhelming, and downright frustrating.

How is an artist or start-up supposed to succeed in heading toward mainstream markets?

There are those who are in the business of selling ideas, that the best system for making sales, gaining followers, and living the high life in a mansion with a fleet of cars is, according to them, practically in everyone's reach!

The key word is practically.

Only, of course, if you watch their video and purchase their system.

Which may or may not be about something that you're passionate about, and that may, or most likely may not, work for you.

Within those businesses, there very well could be those who have a mind that yearns to educate and inform, and make extra money while doing it. Or they could be scams. Whether or not the systems they promote are actually useful or even work, their work is mostly done once a customer signs up. But their system, if real, and if it works for them, may not work for the everyday start up artist or entrepreneur. And one's individuality reigns supreme when making a connection with page followers and converting them into loyal consumers.

The dreamy, mansion filled posts appear to dominate news feeds these days.

They shower promises.

Those individuals flood social media: One Million Followers! Become a Best Seller in 3 days! Gain 25k followers now! Retire as a Millionaire! Write a Best Seller in Days!

This book makes none of those numeric or time based promises. There is no costly system to purchase, no videos to watch for hours on end, just the simple "I" and "How" statements presented in this book, as logically as they can be discussed. There is no further purchase necessary; no expectation of e-mail harvesting or subscriptions.

Just a simple process, a marketing methodology derived from career introspection, presented in the most logical and executable format that I could derive.

This book realizes that it takes years of hard work to establish market penetration with the regular practice of one's craft, combined with targeted and strategic market promotion. This book presents a simple, yet effective philosophy: that connecting with one's followers and converting them into readers, listeners or customers, takes not only a great deal of market analysis, but also a study of and maintenance of the connection once it's established.

And that a true connection will lead to trust, and to sales, if executed with perseverance and purpose.

In the following pages, I will take you on a journey.

It's a journey on the path of marketing, but mostly of connection. I will compare the promotion philosophy that I employ, presenting it against my achievements and missteps. I'm a perpetual student; when something doesn't work, I try something different. I have learned, over the years, that the "throwing mud at the wall" method of marketing, and hoping that something will stick, is really an ineffective way to market.

And I fell into that mud throwing early on in my writing career.

If I had disappointing sales when the book released, I would just start writing the next book. And the next.

And I would say to myself, "This will be the one. I can *feel* it."

By reading this book, you will discover how my page reach (how many people one's posts are reaching on a public page) grew to nearly a half million in approximately seven years. Yes, these numbers do, in fact, translate into sales figures. But that is not the focus of this book.

The focus is connection.

And the connection will bring the sales.

This is not a quick process – but it's effective – and it's mostly organic. It's about connection and maintaining that relationship for the establishment of a true readership; a genuine following, a fan base. And for the writers and musicians: an established base is what gets New York and Hollywood interested in your brand.

There are people out there that will like you and what you are creating. You just have to find them. And the process of doing so should not be seen as overwhelming or intimidating; the process can be easy, quite fun, and can become just as addictive as the new release euphoria that we all have experienced once we have shared our brilliant art with the world.

## *The allure of Social Media*

I hope you all are social media aficionados. If you're not, it's time to get up to speed.

Because as everything currently stands, social media is dictating and revealing the likes and dislikes of consumers day after day and year after year. If you (or your company) are not proficient on social media, the time to build a presence is now: social media brings our companies an avenue of insight, where we can learn about the location, preferences and shopping habits of consumers and how to connect our products with them.

I'm not talking about setting up posts with book cover artwork and a buy link that says "my book is fantastic...it's on a free promotion...please buy it now!"

I am also not talking about sharing meme's complaining that consumers won't pay $2.99 for a Kindle book yet pay $5.00 for a coffee. I see those all of the time. And you know what those pleading posts and complaining memes tell me?

That author isn't selling any books.

Because if they were selling a steady stream of books, they wouldn't have to complain to their social media friends that people would rather pay for a $5.00 coffee rather than $2.99 for a book that the author (hopefully) spent a great deal of time writing, and (hopefully) enlisted professional assistance to ensure a great product and a fantastic read.

I understand the frustration in a lack of sales, but complaining to potential readers about not selling the books doesn't really make the brand attractive. And this book will help the authors and artists who experience an occasional frustration to refocus their energy, and truly become their brand.

Those complaining posts can hurt the professional image, because the professional image should always be that everything is wonderful.

Even if it really isn't.

When discussing one's brand, books are selling like crazy (even if they're not); the brand is doing great (even if it's struggling), and, in fact, the brand is expanding (even if the future currently looks bleak).

Because in promotion, the sky is always blue; it's incessantly filled with rainbows, and people are dancing in fields of lavender in gentle winds, and books are flying off the shelves faster than they can be printed.

Even if they're not.

Because *that* is image.

Promotion is all about presentation.

It's about displaying an impression of success which sends the unspoken message that your bank accounts are overflowing (even if you can scarcely get your bills paid). Perception becomes that the brand is a steady and rousing success. Keeping the rose-tinted glasses on your promotions and follower-connecting posts (see the forthcoming *80/20 Rule*) preserves your image, where your brand is always promoting an image of positivity and success.

A fruitful image has the potential to gain the assumption that your stories *simply must* be fantastic! And it might propel a consumer to click on your ad and take a closer look at your offerings. They can then make their purchase decision based on the merits of your work.

A prosperous image can gain followers and convert them into readers because *prosperity sells*. People are more likely to buy into success – or at least the shared perception of success – rather than sympathetically supporting a desperate author sharing a buy link, or a meme, begging for sales. The would-be-reader clicks on the link, heads to an Amazon page with no reviews and probably zero (or close to it) sales.

What type of perception does that give the would-be-reader?

It could tell them that the book might be inferior, regardless of whether that is true or not. Even some of the more intermediate authors, who share Amazon buy links with a few reviews, are most likely passed over. Especially if they are all five-star reviews, or even some glowing four-star reviews. No book or product will garner all four and five-star reviews. There are going to be people out there who won't connect with the story, or characters. There will be those who didn't like the music, or decided that the product or service doesn't work for them.

While negative reviews can damage one's personal ego, it's important to appreciate that one artist cannot please everyone. Negative reviews give credibility to the product.

If the Amazon page is only populated by a small number of four and five-star reviews, the author or distributor could be manipulating the review process, and then, the reviews might not be trusted. Amazon, also, with its algorithms, has been an increasingly challenging place for leaving genuine reviews, depending on the market. Not every reader of yours may be technologically savvy. If they were given a gift copy for review, send them to Goodreads. Or Barnes and Noble.

And if your book isn't on Barnes and Noble? Make sure to get "expanded distribution" when setting it up for publication.

I've heard authors complain about the reduction of royalties when selling a book via the expanded distribution system. The seller takes their cut. And so does Amazon. So it doesn't leave a whole lot left for the author. Because my brand is global, I sell quite a few books through third party sellers. When those copies sell, I make far less money. However, I always opt for expanded distribution as opposed to an Amazon exclusive. Yes, I take a pay cut with a portion of the books I sell; however, my books and brand gradually become recognized on a global scale, and also garner a more significant search engine presence by my listing them with third party booksellers throughout the world's reading markets. Two of my top 5 markets – India and Brazil – have become reliable sources for regular royalties.

I make far more money in Amazon countries with direct sales; however my volume is higher on alternate selling platforms. My top three markets, the United States of America, the United Kingdom, and Australia, must always be catered to on social media, however other markets have proven significant beyond Amazon.

Still, it doesn't happen quickly.

This is a book about how hard work, patience, and perseverance can better connect an artist with their followers.

How an exploration of insights can define a target market. How aligning a marketing campaign towards the interests of those markets can gain better rewards.

It can work for start-up individuals, seasoned authors, or more established organizations, or it might not work at all. For principles that have worked for me might not work for your specific situation. What I am providing you in this book is my own journey, how it worked for me, and it is up to you, the reader, to apply and adjust the philosophies to your own specific situation.

### *I am my brand. My brand is me.*

It might be considered a cliché for an artist, but the words are telling, and have significant meaning when approaching marketing for any indie artist or start-up entrepreneur. I've often seen creatives over the years work incredibly hard with extraordinary passion to create a book, album, product or service, or another work of art, and then struggle with the marketing process.

I've watched as websites and social media pages are developed to little audiences, if any. And indies in any business have to wear multiple hats. Some are a one-person show, others can employ a small team. But one of the hats that frequently doesn't seem to fit right is the promoter hat.

Yes, we indies have to become excellent promoters.

It doesn't matter if we are writers, vloggers or shop owners. The public doesn't know us, and no matter how elaborate our ultimate goals are, the public needs to be made aware of what we have to offer in order to fall in love with it just a strongly as we have.

To be honest, unless one has a marketing degree, or very deep pockets, the entire promotional process *can* be intimidating, but this book is here to help take the trepidation out of marketing.

When sales trickle in after months, and sometimes years of work, it can prove to be disheartening.

There is a solution to slow flowing sales, however, and it's making a connection. Earning trust, selling indirectly through one's personality and human qualities, makes the artist, but also the brand, relatable.

I have seen far too many indie artists who struggle to gain a few additional followers, make a sale or two, complain in social media groups that the sales simply aren't coming, and either continue with their same unsuccessful process, or simply move on to the next project.

In many cases, creative projects can bring a creative person great joy.

And this book is here to help creatives and entrepreneurs find joy in the building of their own brand; to find joy in building the soaring skyscraper their brand is destined to become, with one carefully laid brick at a time.

We work hard for our passions, and when results aren't the flowing streets of "milk and honey" like we dreamed and imagined, a period of self-doubt is a normal feeling. Heading for some venting and support from friends and peers is also a normal thing to do as well.

Still, I have seen far too many indies give up due to poor sales.

And this book is here to prevent the indies, artists and start-ups from dropping out before their art or product has had a chance. A true chance at success.

This book is here to help you achieve your dreams, in any way it can.

This book is here to help give all indies a boost, regardless of artistic medium or business type, and presents my own marketing methodology compared against my real results.

My successes and my failures.

This philosophy of promotion and connection has helped me triple my overall sales, as well as expand my social media base from just a handful to over 10,000; and, through strategic and well-thought out promotion and advertising, expanded my reach to nearly a half-million in April 2020 [source: Facebook] for the A.L. Mengel page.

I have an 8-step process that I follow for marketing called **the Four "I" Statements, and the Four "How" Statements.** The "I" statements are four things that I know I must employ to work towards reaching my audience and connecting with them; whereas the "How" statements are providing me guidance for my journey. How will I get to where I am going?

And with these statements, I have developed my own system.

## The Four "I" Statements

*I am my brand*

*I must make a connection*

*I can't spend too much time creating the next project*

*I need to spend money to make money*

## The Four "How" Statements

*How I can make a connection*

*How I can tour like a rock star*

*How I can prevent over-marketing*

*How I can collaborate and get to the next step*

*Ones, Twos and Threes*

While I am making no promises that these specific principles will work for everyone, they have been working for me, bit by bit, over time. I have observed that mainstream success can happen for indies in one of three ways, which can classify indies in three categories:

1. **<u>Success can happen seemingly overnight</u>** (think the E.L. James example) where an Indie uploads a Kindle novel that, by chance, sells thousands of copies, attracts the attention of big budget publishing, and then their novel is distributed worldwide; film deals and overflowing bank accounts follow shortly thereafter.

2. **<u>Success can happen over time</u>** after a well-established indie is discovered once a significant readership foundation is built over the course of years: think Hugh Howey. This can be a highly coveted position to be in, but still rare.

3.  **Success can happen over many years**, in small steps, which can lead to ups and downs of elation and frustration, but usually, after many years, one can look back and begin to measure the slow and gradual market penetration and fanbase construction. I believe that the majority of indies fall into this category, but dream of being #1's.

I am a #3, and I would imagine that the target readers of this book are #3's too. While I cannot promise that the "I" and "How" method will fast-track your own product and brand platform mix to mainstream success, and catapult you to a #2, or maybe even a #1, I can certainly attest to the growth of my own brand. Am I destined to be discovered by the mainstream market? Who knows. Only time will tell. But I believe that if I apply the principles in this book on a regular and ongoing basis, the journey towards a more substantial market presence will continue. I have been mentioning that my social media base has grown from just a handful of followers to over 10,000, and my sales have increased year to year, with the largest increase thus far in 2018, when sales more than doubled.

I am able to measure my success, and make myself the promise that my work will endure. A measure of success, I believe, is critical for any start-up writer, artist, musician or entrepreneur. A measure of success must always be present, whether its via sales or a base of loyal followers. Those aspects can offer insight if the direction you are headed in is the right one. While Facebook pages have insights for business models, sales data must also be analyzed in tandem from different sources (example, Amazon) to determine the advertising versus sales correlation.

Regardless of the speed, I've grown over the past decade. I'm not mainstream yet, but I aspire to be within another ten years. Market penetration takes time, patience and a continuous effort. It's enormously important to maintain insight into one's own journey to prevent discouragement.

## *Earn their trust: follow the 80/20 rule*

The page followers are the golden arc of the covenant.

You must protect them; you must stand up for their interests, and you must earn their trust. This is not something that will happen overnight, but if a page owner follows the "80/20 rule" of social media posting, your page followers may gradually make the connection and learn to trust.

But that isn't a promise, it's an assumption.

The reality of marketing is that sometimes, the connection just simply doesn't happen. Regardless of following all of the principles. Sometimes the followers just don't connect. Sometimes they never become readers. But using these principles will greatly increase the *chances* of a connection.

The 80/20 rule of marketing is also known as the "Pareto Principle" which indicates that 80% of sales come from 20% of customers. A savvy social media marketer needs to keep the Pareto Principle in mind at all times when posting to their page, and always remember the 20% of your followers who are actually buying your books.

The 80/20 principle when applied to social media posting is quite simple: the philosophy is that 80 percent of the posts should be something relatable to the page followers. Marketing and sales related posts should only comprise 20 percent of the posts, at the maximum. In addition, of those posts, consideration for the 20% of your followers who are actually readers is important. Gaining insight from the page analytics is crucial to determine what demographic is connecting and engaging with your page.

And then, the posts must be tailored to what your followers like. When I started uploading and sharing videos, I noticed that the views were increasing. In addition, the video views seemed to spike for two types of videos: book trailers, and videos of me discussing a writing related topic.

Those analytics told me that my page followers were on my page because they were interested in my work as an author (which makes sense). I also deduced that the page followers liked to see me on video, particularly speaking about creative and writing ventures. The views for those videos soared, and I saw numbers that

I had yet to see at that time: videos in the hundreds, and eventually, in the thousands of views. So I was gradually finding a way to connect, and that was through video.

### *Find a 'Hook' and don't be afraid to create a "sub" brand*

I know *I* don't like to be "sold" to. I like to make my purchasing decisions based on the merits of the product, or in the case of a book, I like to know a little something about the author. I very rarely read a book from an author I have never heard of. I would imagine that a number of others feel the same way.

Am I correct or is that statement far-reaching?

Regardless of how much of a masterpiece your creative work may be in your eyes, you still have to hook the people into your brand in order for *them* to fall in love with your product.

On the social media pages that I follow, I see all ends of the marketing spectrum. Generally speaking, if I am scrolling through my news feed, and I see a "buy my book" ad from an author who I may or may not know, I typically will keep scrolling. I do this unless the book seems extraordinary, then I may take a closer look. That's rare, however.

If I see a "buy my book" ad from an author that I know, I almost always will take a closer look. Because I know that author in one form or another, it sparks a curiosity inside me which compels me to take a closer look and see what they have written. And, in some cases, I have bought the book from an author that I know, because the offering is strong enough that it is compelling and has merit.

But it's important to point out that I have, almost never, purchased a book from a "buy my book" ad from an author that I don't know in one form or another, simply because they put up a sponsored post declaring their book as the greatest the world has seen in years.

So is that fair to the authors that I've scrolled past?

It's time to put things into perspective.

Generally, when I scroll past, there are a number of reasons why. I can always appreciate a professionally designed cover, and a compelling story, but there are numerous professionally designed covers and compelling stories being marketed by authors around the world every single day. If a random sponsored post appears on my news feed, I might have been part of their target market.

Or I may even follow their page.

But if I don't "know" them, at least through a sense of their social media presence and personality, I have no sense of who they are, and why should I care about their book?

I'm not going to jump through hoops to look through their page, see what they've been posting, and decide if I like them as a person, when, on the other hand, there's an author I know because they are posting things that connect with me on a regular basis, and they're marketing an equally compelling book with a professionally designed cover as well.

Which author should I choose to support?

My philosophy may sound harsh, but it's common. An author who is insistent with selling posts on their page will fail to connect with their followers who don't know them. An author who fails to personalize their posts in a humanistic fashion will struggle to connect on a individual level. And then that author just becomes "some machine" behind the page, and without a connection, the element of caring is lost.

Hiding behind mistargeted advertising causes a failure to connect with one's page following, and can inhibit sales growth. The challenging part is finding ways to connect with the audience.

A Facebook page needs advertising, from the moment its created. People need to know that your page, your brand, and your products are all there for the offering. An interesting page ad with a "hook" statement drawing people to the page to view compelling content will increase the chances of a page like from that individual.

Now, what do I mean about a "hook" statement?

It really shares the same philosophy when creating an opening scene for a book, a blurb/teaser, a tagline…all of those principles.

It's a short statement that draws people in.

I knew, years ago, that my author page needed an identity through which I could hook people to the page and gain their following.

And that is how #TheWritingStudio hashtag was born.

I had in my mind that in "The Writing Studio", all were welcome. Creativity would always be embraced. There would always be an encouraging environment, and it would be a place where creativity would be supported and proclaimed in a positive way.

And so #TheWritingStudio became a "sub-brand" of the overall A.L. Mengel umbrella. Over time, with the use of the created hashtag, Google searches were populated and "The Writing Studio" established itself as a significant force in A.L. Mengel branding, where topics would populate internet searches just by searching for the hashtag.

Over the subsequent years, I created another hashtag, called #MusicfromTheWritingStudio. This was in approximately 2014. At that point in time, I had not yet learned much about my followers, and I didn't have a significant amount of followers on the A.L. Mengel Facebook page at that point anyway.

But I knew I had a passion for music. It turns out some of my page followers do as well.

Music has had a great influence on my own creativity, and I have always believed that music is the universal language of the world. It brings people together from different backgrounds and cultures and can speak to, and through, the soul.

Depending on how you choose to present your own brand, the types of hashtags that you employ, and what type of posts you make and share, will determine if your audience feels a connection with you or not.

Looking back at the 80/20 rule of social media posting, it is important to remember that ratio, that 80 percent of the posts should be making an effort to connect with and to engage with the audience. No matter the size. Only 20 percent (at the most) should be marketing and sales related.

And I am not talking about posting about one homogenous topic.

If you like cat videos and want to share one, great. Some of your page followers may share that same interest with you. And even better – if you have a book with a feline character – then discreet market pairing can take place.

The act of placing a buy link in a post about a different topic, chosen to relate to one's page followers, must be a seldom occurrence, but if done sparingly, can be effective. The pairing post can hook the follower in. Your reflections on the post spark an interest. And then a discreet mention of your book or other product might spark some interest for a closer look.

A few years ago, NASA had blasted the news to the world that their satellite "Juno" had reached Jupiter's orbit in July of 2016. At that point in time, I was writing *War Angel,* and my science fiction debut, *The Wandering Star,* had been released a few months prior, in March.

It's important to mention is that I saw the news story and the light bulb illuminated in my head to promote *The Wandering Star* in conjunction with sharing the news from NASA on my page.

Now, remember the 80/20 rule.

On that very early morning in July, I opened up my personal news feed and discovered the story – not because it was already all over the news – as it was still dark in the eastern United States. I saw the announcement relatively early on, because I made it a point to follow NASA's page when *The Wandering Star* went into publication.

And so by the time the elation of Juno's arrival into Jupiter's Orbit was all over the news, and by the time my news feed had begun to fill with amateur newscasters (my friends) announcing the news, I already had a post about it on my author page, with a call to action, linking my science fiction debut which, conveniently, had a sequence in the story directly related to Jupiter and its moons, which I discussed in the post.

I'm not claiming to be able to predict the future, and part of the success and timing of the ad really could have had a stroke of luck within it. As I am a firm believer in the technique of gradual build-up versus gradual build-down in bringing a product to market, I decided it would be important to follow specific scientific related websites and social media pages, one of them being NASA, while preparing the book release.

I didn't know at the time that Juno was closing in on Jupiter's orbit; that is where the stroke of luck came in for me.

A savvy marketer will follow a variety of topics, particularly those which could somehow relate back to their product, in one way or another. I have made potential market pairing page follows part of my production process, for each project. I conduct research on various topics that could be related to the project, even if just loosely, to possibly employ some market pairing down the road.

### *Embrace your own principles*

In the 2015 book *#Writestorm*, the principle that remained with me the most was this philosophy:

*Be a doer. Not a dreamer. And by doing, you have the power to achieve your dreams.*

That is a quite specific principle that *#Writestorm* embraces. How can one expect enthralling sales if the period after a book is released – which is extraordinarily critical to market penetration – is essentially ignored?

There are differences between doers and dreamers.

While *#Writestorm* touches on the differences between the two personalities in a creative writing perspective, this book compares the two marketing personalities.

Marketing doers versus marketing dreamers.

A marketing dreamer will have the same elation on release day that a marketing doer will have, but there is a key difference between the two personalities. If sales come slow, and they often do, especially for indie authors or artists, the dream can easily seem deflated. Whereas one's creative project, in many cases, has taken months or possibly years of blood, sweat and tears, and much emotion, the public has no idea that this project even existed.

And when the marketing dreamer's bubble deflates, when the sales trickle in, sometimes from family or friends, they quickly move to the next project in search of the book release high once again.

A marketing doer sees the dismal results and takes action.

They take action not by plastering pleading posts to buy their book on social media, but by sitting down, and analyzing *why* the book or album may not be selling, by studying their audience. When I transformed from a dreamer into a doer, things started to change for me.

I will be completely honest with you.

It took several years to start to see a turnaround. But it happened. And the *#Writestorm* process, and its philosophies, had quite a significant part of that for me by transforming my own creative and marketing self from a dreamer…into a doer.

*#Writestorm*, the first book in this series, had introduced a writing process which authors immediately embraced as a way out of writer's block. When I saw how many imitators which had surfaced in the years after the book's release, I initially let out a chuckle. I felt flattered that other writers believed in the process as well, even if they had tweaked the one, true *#Writestorm* process and made it work for them.

The *#Writestorm* process outlines a methodology of short, focused writing "power hours". *#Writestorm* had already been out and in use for years when the imitations started to surface. I thought to myself, interesting similarity. In some cases, the process was tweaked and renamed. Initially, I felt somewhat violated. I thought to myself, what the heck? I put in all this work to develop a process that works and then people snatch it away, tweak it, and market a new, renamed process as their own?

But one of the key things that the imitators failed to realize, was that *#Writestorm* is far more than just a simple writing power hour.

And that is what has set it apart from the copycats. It's a creative philosophy that not only carves a way through writer's block, but embraces a proven methodology of managing one's time and space to gain much needed productivity in that "power hour."

And that's why the process commanded a book.

I called my representatives, and they were ready to call their copyright contacts. And then I stopped. No one else was claiming to call their process *#Writestorm*. After thinking about it, I thought again of the old saying: imitation is the fondest form of flattery. When others were out there copying the *#Writestorm* process, I studied the copycats. And despite similarities, it wasn't the exact process. Changes were made and others marketed a tweaked process of their own.

And suddenly, I became more positive. "There's a marketing opportunity in there," I told myself.

I truly was flattered that what I'd brought to the writing community – and, in particular, the indie author community – was being practiced, at least to a degree, in some form. As the creator of the original, I felt proud, as if I had made a contribution to the community in a positive way. And while the book has received mostly positive reviews, there is the occasional one-star.

And that confirmed to me that the process doesn't work for everybody.

I remembered the philosophy on reviews: that one-star reviews give a product credibility. We all know that no one can please everyone all of the time; no product is perfect for all. And no process will work for everyone that tries it.

I felt though, that the *#Writestorm* process needed a resurgence. There was a marketing opportunity brought forth by the imitators.

I knew, back in 2015, when the book *#Writestorm* was written over the course of a single week, sent for editing, and released, that to protect the true *#Writestorm* process as the original, the process needed a copyright. I knew, in more recent months, that the writing community needed to be reminded of *#Writestorm* methodology.

And so a campaign was launched called:

ALWAYS THE ORIGINAL.

ALWAYS WORKS.

ALWAYS THE BEST.

NEVER COMPROMISE.

It was critical, at least in my own mind, that *#Writestorm* needed a new stake added to its claim: it was the original, and while the imitations over the years had indeed been flattering, the *#Writestorm* process was quite specific; it's a creative method, and it works. People needed to be reminded of that.

The always/never formulation of the campaign uses the power of suggestion: it suggests that there are, in fact, other "writing sprint" versions of *#Writestorm* out there, but that they aren't the original. And the campaign also implies that if a writer were to latch onto an imitator, then, in some fashion, they would be selling themselves short, and possibly missing out on something important which resides within the original.

And they would be.

I knew *#Writestorm* needed a further reach, a rebirth of sorts.

I was holding my own personal *#Writestorm* sessions back in 2014, but it wasn't until 2015 when the creative method received some international attention. I participated in an event that I happened to see, by chance, on a Facebook group called 'The #Awethors'. It was a *Cover Wars* event, which is an online gathering of writers and those who appreciate them. Authors submit their best book covers and participants can vote on the covers which they like. The covers with the most likes advance to the next round, and so on, and so forth.

I was thrilled to participate because I had just hired a new designer…and the covers I entered, I felt, were a perfect representation of my artistic vision and my brand.

And that, I found, was critical.

### *Your brand is art and the art is the brand*

I've made some good decisions over the years while working as a published author, and some not so good ones. But one of the best decisions I ever made was to hire a professional designer who really understood my branding. I consider myself lucky for finding the graphic artist that I did, it was as if it were mere luck, but it also could have been destiny, and written in the stars.

I've seen the work of other artists over the years, and much of it has been impressive. But I always remained loyal to my designer, who has illustrated my covers since 2014's *The Quest for Immortality*, through the two 'Colonia' novels of 2019: *The Arrival of Destiny* and *Battle of the Trinity,* as well as the cover for the book you are currently reading. All of the covers in-between those two periods were designed by this particular designer as well.

By keeping the same designer, there has been a continual sense of branding. She has held a deep understanding of what visions I want to translate. Each of my covers' artwork is original and represents a scene from the story or represents the story thematically. In addition, she understands my brand. Although each of my covers are strikingly different, they each share, at least artistically, a similar brand feel.

The consistency with the artwork over the years has also helped me understand my branding, which has proven helpful since I have been progressing with two media avenues: graphic design and video production. The consistency in the art representation of the brand has helped carve my own artistic understanding of my brand, which has assisted me in maintaining the brand style in artwork and videos that I create myself for promotion.

As for cover production, I tend to start working with my designer on covers very early on in the writing process, which, I have found, is rather unorthodox. I've observed that many other authors reveal their book covers a short period before release. I, on the other hand, practice gradual build-up marketing, which I believe is important in creating a buzz surrounding the release. I know that I need my artwork relatively early on in the writing process so the marketing effort can commence.

I do this for two reasons.

One, translating my vision to the designer helps me better understand the story, its characters, and the journey in each book.

And two, it provides me with official promotional artwork so I can set up a long-running marketing campaign of the book, which adds some creative pressure, especially if I am writing under deadline with an active pre-order.

The artwork, however, really helped me understand my branding, for I am a visual learner. Always have been. I remember those standardized reading comprehension tests from my school days. Sometimes, I would struggle with them.

Who would have ever thought then that I was destined to write critically acclaimed novels?

Anyway, time reveals destiny, and I have always thought of myself to be a perpetual student.

I remember when I was still working as a manager in the hospitality industry, I took a training class on branding. It discussed the philosophy of "being the brand". And that philosophy remained with me over the years, and easily paired with my college education from Philadelphia. My education has provided me a better understanding of marketing, promotion and all of the different aspects that go along with it.

But it's taken me years to fully understand the branding philosophy, and to come to realize that, as an author, I am my brand. The brands aren't my books, or my characters, or even my t-shirts, posters or handbags.

My brand is me.

*I* am the brand.

And this rings true not only for authors, but for musicians, artists and other creatives.

Before people will buy what you are offering, they first have to buy into YOU.

When one puts themselves into the mindset of an author, artist, musician or start-up entrepreneur, the simple brilliance of this advice rings true for all.

People are personal creatures.

I don't know about your specific preferences, but I don't like to be "told" to do something by some anonymous entity hiding behind an advertisement – I'd rather know a little something about who (or what) is telling me that this product is the next greatest thing to sliced bread.

Everyone may not agree with me, and I understand that side of the coin as well.

There may be some people out there who trust certain brands, and people will, in most cases, buy into whatever that trusted brand or person is attempting to sell them.

But in my case, and I also imagine the case of countless other Indies out there in the marketplace, if it's an author, artist, musician or start-up entrepreneur, I want to know a little about them and their own philosophies so I can rally behind them and help them – and their brand – succeed and get to the next level.

So, my creative friends, it's important to be your brand.

Say it with me: *I am my brand. When people buy into me, and earn my trust, they will start to buy my products.*

But there is something quite important to remember. Think back to those empty promises from the beginning of the book.

One Million Followers! 25,000 likes in three days! And so on and so forth.

Those who clog your news feed with those type of promises are simply selling dreams and collecting money. Because dreamers are an interesting bunch. We will try anything to achieve our dreams. But in reality, what it really takes is time. And a lot of hard work, perseverance, combined with a will to succeed.

There's no proven hot-shot plan, there's no golden ticket. It's about relationship building. And that, my friends, takes time, work and energy.

### The value of the brand: The price/value relationship

I rarely hold free promotions of my writing. Sometimes I do, but it's usually for a strategically placed campaign. *Ashes*, which has supernatural and paranormal themes, was offered on a free promotion recently over the Easter weekend.

I opted to choose the "Special Edition" Kindle version for the promotion for two reasons. One, use of the word "special" helps in selling copies. Also, with a list price of $8.99 for the Kindle, getting it free for a three day period was a bargain!

*Ashes Special Edition* rose up the free charts on Amazon, and I was happy to see the great numbers rolling in, even if I didn't make a cent on the "sales".

I was simply casting my wider net for new readers.

All authors need to do that occasionally.

And there is nothing wrong with an occasional freebie for audience building, but those promotions must be strategically placed and targeted. No author or start-up creative can afford to take the risk of cheapening the brand.

I chose Easter weekend because historically, during that time of year, a certain percentage of the population tend to have spiritual thoughts. And it often takes the identification of how the public might be perceiving life during a certain time period to strategically place promotions.

During the springtime, Christians are thinking about their beliefs; pagans and Wiccans are preparing to celebrate Ostara, the Jewish population is thinking about their Passover beliefs, and the general population is thinking about flowers, renewal, a new year, productivity, etc.

And then there are different times of the year for different promotions that appeal to readers of other genres.

Do you remember in the previous pages, when NASA's space probe Juno was reaching Jupiter in the Jovian system? It was big news. I immediately put my science fiction on promotion, and started posting about Juno. And NASA. Not necessarily about my books. (Remember the 80/20 rule: it's coming.)

In order for a promotion to be successful, several key elements must be in place.

One, the target for the promotion needs to be clearly defined. In the case of the *Ashes Special Edition*, the target was fairly broad, so I was predicting a large reach, however also predicting less engagement with the post, considering that it was being marketed to such a large audience.

While my philosophy was to "blast" the title out there, like throwing a handful of fish bait in a lake, and hoping there might be a bite or two, it's not always the best if the goal is direct sales. In the case of this promotion, I went against my own philosophy of having a strategic, targeted promotion and I did that for one reason only.

The title was being offered for free, and the only time I will allow myself to do that is in a "blast". In a more targeted promotion, where direct sales measure the success, brings us to number two: the promotion needs to be long-running.

It's been proven that people generally will "mull-over" something several times before finally making a decision to purchase, and the case is no different in a book, a piece of art or music, or a new product. Some consumers read reviews, others seek to see if anyone they know has already read the book or used the product. In the meantime, the book/product makes its way down their news feed once again to remind them of the product. There is a delicate balance to this, as people can quickly become disinterested if they see the book/product too little…or too much.

# TWO

**I MUST MAKE A CONNECTION BEFORE MAKING SALES.**

THE ABOVE STATEMENT IS PROBABLY something that many might disagree with me on. And other artists and entrepreneurs, please keep in mind that I am an author, and writing this from an author's perspective. But these common sense marketing principles that I have absorbed over the years can also be applied to your own specific medium.

So is the statement at the start of this chapter bad advice?

It depends on one's interpretation.

We're all at different stages of our creative careers, but, I would imagine, if you are reading this book, we are probably all on a similar ship. And, when I published my first novel in 2013, *Ashes*, I thought I was in First Class.

I was astoundingly excited.

I was elated. I had removed a personal barrier that had been holding me back for years.

My writing, it seems, from analysis over the years, and from the 2019 introspective video series *#TheEraOf*, was very personal, even if I didn't realize that while writing. Each book I released appeared to be a stepping stone to the next era of my life, and had drawn from me personally far more than I thought it had.

When I was preparing to release *Ashes*, I had to remove a very real, and very specific barrier to my own progress. I was afraid of what people would think about my story. I had to overcome my fear of rejection. It took me about a year of editing and rewrites to get *Ashes* to a point where I was happy with the project, and ready to release it.

I was so happy that I took that personal step in my life and mustered up the courage to share my first novel, which I had been working on for years. The story was in my head, probably, since the 1990's, and, as I published it, I hoped for the best. I was an excited first-time author filled with the fuel of dreams.

How did I clear that creative hurdle?

That's hard to put into words.

I threw myself into the work and reviewed it countless times, over years, and then I asked myself one question.

How bad do I want this?

At that point, I'd been telling myself for two decades that I wanted to be a novelist, and that moment was my chance.

The door was open.

I asked myself: Am I going to go through it? Or am I going to give up on the dream?

And I knew, deep within my heart and soul, that giving up was *not* an option. For being a writer, to me, is a calling. In my opinion, it's a similar, soulful calling to be an artist. Or musician. Or even an entrepreneur.

We are special.

We have a drive that some others don't.

We take the risks while others opt for security. In many cases, we don't know when our next payday is going to be. All creatives, especially the indies, are entrepreneurs in a sense.

And entrepreneurs are those risk-takers; some of whom have built the world as we know it, and, in many cases, helped carry it into the next era, creating a global culture.

Do you think if Bill Gates had not followed his dream in his garage, that the world would be the same as it is today? If Stephen King's wife didn't fish the manuscript for *Carrie* out of the trash can, would we have so much cultural influence and art?

Sure, we would.

Someone would have done it.

Others would have cleared the barriers to their own progress in pursuing their own dreams. And for all of you reading this, it's important to remember that your creative work — your own contribution — has the potential to *change the world*.

Bill Gates and Stephen King were destined to be the harbingers of change and influence across the world.

And so could you.

My barrier, however, was real.

I was worried about what people would think about my writing, and if I even had the talent to be an actual published author: *Ashes* had been rejected by New York agents time and time again over years. Little did I know in 2008-2009 that the story was ahead of its time. During the years when I was knocking on New York's door, *Twilight* was all the rage, and mainstream publishers weren't looking for more stories similar to those at the time.

While **The Tales of Tartarus** books aren't similar to *Twilight* except for being supernatural, New York didn't want those type of books at the time. I didn't have the crystal ball in those days to tell me that New York would become interested in stories of immortals again in the late 2010's.

I opted to publish it on my own, through my own imprint, Parchman's Press.

My heart pounded in my chest as I uploaded the first Kindle partial to Amazon in April of 2013, and then, I could call myself a published author. In the course of the next few months, I gained some confidence, and released the follow-up partial, month by month, on Kindle, in the format of a "serial novel".

I received extraordinary marketing advice to split the novel into its four partials and release them in close succession, as individual titles. Four titles, quadruple the royalties.

### *How "First Novel Syndrome" can inhibit growth*

I gained quite a bit of confidence when experiencing support from friends and family who were elated that I had published works. They bought the books, reviewed them, and stroked my ego, which prepared me for the ultimate release: my first paperback novel.

*Ashes* clocked in at around 109,000 words, 350 pages in a 6x9 format, and I finally...*finally!*...held the book in my hands for the first time. Each moment of my life seemed to lead up to that moment.

When the giant box arrived at the doorstep, I tore it open, tossed the brown paper packaging to the side, and feasted my eyes upon the beauties: 25 pristine copies of *Ashes*.

I was finally a published author! I had created something which would live longer than me!

Other authors had told me that the "real work" started once the book headed into print, but I was soaring through the clouds, too high to hear them. In the subsequent years, I had joined a multitude of online writers' groups, eager to share my new knowledge!

I was a creative genius in my own eyes; I had achieved something that few do. I had written a novel, to completion, was collecting supportive reviews, and the sky was the limit! I knew – I just *knew* then – that at any moment, the big New York publishers would be sending me an email. They'd be so astounded at the amazingness of the novel they'd passed on – and could they republish it?

It's utterly magnificent!

The emails never came, but I remained on cloud 9 for quite a while.

I had quickly become a recognized name in the online writer's groups, starting conversations and chats which gained quite a bit of comments and even some controversy: "This A.L. Mengel has written one novel. I have been writing for a decade. Who is he to tell me how to construct a story and publish and market a book? His page only has a handful of followers!"

I made some missteps shortly after *Ashes* went into print because I had something which some authors have: first novel syndrome.

There are some that believe that this concept is that the first novel of a series doesn't measure up to the subsequent books. At least that's the "official" definition according to a Google search. However, my own definition varies: it's when a newly published indie author becomes "all knowledgeable" after releasing their first creative work.

And rightfully so, because it *is* an achievement.

Even if a creative only releases a single work in their lifetime, it's still a milestone.

So it's a reason to celebrate, regardless of whether that author or artist continues to release novels for years and decades, or decides to retire after that single work: the story has been told!

But what I had forgotten after *Ashes* headed into print, and received positive reviews, was that I was still a student. And learning.

I'm still a student now, in 2020, as I am writing this. I have learned that, while I have made strides in the maturation of my writing over the years, and also developed my knowledge of the publication business, there is *always* room for improvement. Despite how often I feel like a mentor, there are other times where I realize that, in many situations, I am still a protégé.

In the face of my grand leap of publication, in late 2013 and early 2014, there were many others that I interacted with who had many more years of experience than I did. They had published many more novels, had more followers and fans, readers and reviews. They had better engagement, and I was there, as the newbie, telling them how it was "supposed" to be done.

And that, to me, is first novel syndrome from a marketing perspective.

It took me a few years to shed that perceived arrogance, and to realize that, despite my accomplishments, regardless of those who reminded me that I had talent, that my storytelling style was unique and destined for greatness, that I was still a student of the business.

And the craft.

My storytelling style was my own, but I had no idea then of what it would become in terms of maturity in my prose.

And when it came to the business side of writing, at that time, I didn't realize that I had quite a bit still to learn as well.

So, back to the topic at hand.

### Aces in their places

I was told, early in my writing career, that once book one is out in the public, it's immediately time to write book two. Because book two sells book one. And then after that, its immediately time to write book three. Because book three sells book two, and so on and so forth.

I completely understand and appreciate this time-proven philosophy.

However, I have found, that employing a *different* marketing philosophy, based on a fusion of ideas from different creative fields (besides writing) that book one *can* sell on its own if it's given the proper marketing time, promotion, and allowed to flourish and find its readers. This philosophy, of course, makes several assumptions.

It presumes that the book is well written. That the story and characters are compelling, and the topic is what the reading public wants at the time. The viewpoint also assumes that the book was professionally produced, professionally edited, and professionally formatted with a professionally designed cover.

I don't think I used the word professionally enough.

Because I cannot stress that if the product is not professionally produced, then this book and this process is useless.

It takes a creative team to produce a work of art, believe it or not.

One author shows, and the do-it-yourselfers are admired for their versatility; however, one person simply cannot be the expert in all areas.

On my creative team, I am the storyteller.

That is my area of expertise. An old saying goes, "Aces in their places."

The position of storyteller is my ace position.

Do I have the ability to self-edit or design my own cover? Sure. Would I have an inferior product as a result? Most likely. Would I see it? Probably not. I, like many others, are biased to my own work. It's always beautiful and wonderful in my own eyes, as it should be. And if I were to be a one-author show, the market might perceive my work a tad differently than I would. I simply don't have the same connection, don't feel the same energy, etc.

But when a book releases and doesn't live up to the author's expectations, what could be the reason if it was professionally produced as per literary standards? If the cover is striking and professional and says "New York" when viewing it, why didn't the would-be readers pick it up simply based on that, if a cover were supposed to sell a book?

Maybe the story is not what the market wants at the time. Consider *Ashes*.

Previously I had mentioned that *Twilight* had just been all the rage. Still, *Ashes* had a respectable release. I opted then to dive into the next three books. But had I known back then what I know now, marketing wise, I probably would have made a different decision.

And so I studied how other artists promote, namely musicians: a musical artist or band has a rotation where they have touring years versus years they create new music. There is a buildup to the album release over time and singles are released and promoted strategically: usually intermittently over weeks or months leading up to the release of the full album.

Shortly after the release of the full album, usually, a tour is announced. Some time passes when the show is being assembled and rehearsed, and then the tour schedule begins.

When I was studying this approach to creative marketing in the music business, I was wondering how this could be applied to writing. I compared the businesses and wondered how an author, particularly an indie author, could execute a "gradual buildup" marketing technique prior to release; how they could release a book, plan a long-running book tour, and wear the promoter hat to SUCCESS the following year.

## *Gradual build-up versus Gradual build-down*

This altering concept to the indie author norm was proven after the 2017 release of *The Mortician*. The novel project had multiple delays during production, and the supernatural/horror themed story was released a single week before Christmas.

Who the *heck* is going to want to read a supernatural thriller in the Christmas season?

Despite that, *The Mortician* proceeded to become my most successful release of all time, all while dealing with a subject matter that people, in a lot of cases, are either drawn to out of curiosity, or run away from: funeral homes, grieving, embalming, and the mystery of the afterlife.

The success of *The Mortician* was quite simple: it was given time to flourish and find its readers.

In addition, there was a gradual build-up in promotion before the book was even written. I released a video in May of 2017 detailing how I had had a chilling experience while conducting research for the book in a cemetery. Yes, the chilling experience *actually* happened. Its paramount to maintain honesty with potential readers and build a level of trust. With the release of that first video, there was already a nice amount of people who were aware of my new book project before I had even written a word.

And that created two things for me. One, I got excited about the project. My sci-fi release for that year, *The Europa Effect* hadn't even released yet, and I was already talking, on my social media channels, about "going back to my roots", which, in my mind, was heading back to supernatural storytelling.

I got some excitement after announcing that I would be heading back to my roots from the readers of my first series, **The Tales of Tartarus**. I hadn't marketed to those readers directly since *War Angel* went into print nearly a full year prior, as I had focused my efforts on promoting my science fiction series, **The Vega Chronicles**.

My science fiction reader base was excited for *The Europa Effect*, and now, with the release of a simple video, readers of my supernatural series were getting excited as well…even if the release of *The Mortician* was still nearly ten months away.

And two, it prepared me for the marketing journey – the gradual build-up – that I would take leading up to the release of the novel:

I created several different book trailers which each touched on a different aspect of the story. There was a short, overall teaser (released in late 2016), a theme trailer, a character trailer, and a plot trailer, all released in succession over the course of eleven months leading up to the release of *The Mortician*.

### Sometimes you don't need to write

In 2018, the following year, I did not write or release a novel. Instead, I embarked on a book tour, which I will be covering in much more detail in a later chapter of this book.

*The Mortician* was the headlining book on this tour, and it received national attention. During the course of the tour, Readers' Favorite gave the story a Five Star review. I participated in interviews, which promoted not only that novel, but the novels that I'd already released up to that point. Once the tour was over, sales doubled for that year. *The Mortician* quickly became my most successful release, and my other novels were selling more copies as well. *The Mortician* represents a turning point in my writing career: I decided to tackle a topic that I thought many people would shy away from; I was wrong.

And when the story was analyzed by reviewers, and after receiving questions from those who'd read the novel, it opened my eyes:

I really wrote *The Mortician* for myself.

And it was my most personal story that I'd released to date.

I would have never learned that creative lesson had I simply opted to dive into the next novel in early 2018. In January of 2018, I was on a productive roll. With *The Mortician* just released, I had decided to take a gamble on the knowledge that I'd picked up studying the music business.

I had paired up with fellow author Jeremy Croston, and we decided to join forces for the tour; he had just released his critically acclaimed novel *Malice of the Cross* on the same day as *The Mortician*, and we considered them sister projects.

We planned the tour together, and went live on feeds together on our Facebook pages. We were surprised those feeds received thousands of views – **little did I know at the time that this was a very important future marketing clue for me**. I was also writing a new novel which came to me in a dream after coming off of research for *The Mortician*.

But then, suddenly, just two weeks before the *#TakeAJourney2018* Book Tour was scheduled to kick off in a scheduled event in Orlando, my aunt died.

And while the tour remained on schedule due to all of the parties involved, my writing project did a complete 180 degree turn.

I was learning then, slowly, that it was necessary to let a recently released novel find its audience and grow. Maybe it took my aunt passing away to teach me that lesson: don't spend too much time working on the next novel.

Because the project that was just released to the world needs to grow some wings to flourish. And grow. And find its readers.

If the author will let it.

And so, I put the new project on which I had been working on the back burner. I was saddened by the death of my aunt, but also excited about the tour. I released a video on my author page telling my Beloved Friends the news of my aunt's death **(another marketing clue).**

And then, I had an unexpected eureka moment.

I was on the phone with Jeremy and told him how my aunt loved my science fiction. And that I felt **The Vega Chronicles** (the science fiction series) needed to continue. I told him that it was planned to be an epic read. I was inspired by my aunt's love of my science fiction stories, and told him that the book was going to be too big for a 5x8 format. So Jeremy suggested releasing it in two volumes.

And then *Colonia* was born.

The two novels, I knew at the time, would be far too encompassing to write fully while on tour with *The Mortician.* Yet after the February events, I started both *The Arrival of Destiny* and *Battle of the Trinity* and wrote as much as I could while on the two-month tour break.

The tour had a date at a comic-book based store and bar called 'Gods and Monsters' on February 28, 2018, and after that, the break was until April 3, 2018. Perfect. Plenty of time to write the beginnings of both novels, I thought.

"I want to release both novels on the same day," I told Jeremy on the phone. "They're both one story, and they have to be written and released at the same time."

"Well, if there's anyone that can pull that off, it's A.L. Mengel," Jeremy said.

Jeremy gave me a much appreciated boost of confidence, and I went to work on both stories, but I was stalling. The next date of the tour was looming, and I was busier than expected promoting upcoming tour dates, and the headlining book, *The Mortician*.

April came, and for the tour event, Jeremy and I conducted an *#AuthorsDiscussionGroup* event where we discussed 'Breaking Out of the Indie Bubble'. At that point the book tour was heading national, and Jeremy's leg was over, so now I was on my own.

### *Don't overestimate energy for ego*

My *Colonia* double-novel project was calling, but it was sitting in the background for the most part, while I focused on the tour. May through September 2018 was a rather busy schedule for me which required air and sea travel, so very little work was done on any new writing. *The Mortician* took center stage for *#BookOnABench* drops and readings in various states. I even did a scene exploration live feed on my Facebook page in Philadelphia (the exact location in the story where characters met) and nearly fell down the stairs on live video!

But I made a huge mistake with *Colonia*.

I announced to the world, in the form of a trailer, that the novels would release together in October of 2018. And it's important to consider here: a trailer is a huge powerhouse of a marketing tool which leads up to a book release, but it also becomes a quasi-promise once a date is added. After a trailer is released and promoted, there are would-be readers out there expecting the release once the trailer is dated.

I over-estimated my creative energy for 2018.

I had embarked on an all-encompassing tour, and little did I know, the *Colonia* novels wouldn't actually gain momentum in writing until early 2019. Four months after I had told my readers that they would have been released. I sheepishly made a post on my page letting my followers know that *Colonia* would be delayed.

During the promotional run for *The Mortician*, I simply did not have the time to work on a massive writing project, and if I had made time, even via *#Writestorm*, then the promotion of *The Mortician* would have suffered greatly. The book would not have achieved the amazing results that it did. I had to shed the archaic philosophy of jumping immediately to the next writing project.

Lesson learned.

That's when I saw that books need a significant promotional run, which I liken to a marketing build-down period. There is a period post release when the author is required to go out and let the readers know that the book is out, that the pages are filled with blood, sweat and tears, and that there's no better time to read the book.

While a book tour is an ideal method for the marketing build down period, tours can prove daunting for the indie author.

But not impossible.

As a reminder, book tours will be covered in a later chapter of this book in detail. Regardless of the ability to tour, and the creative "outside the box" ways that are presented in the chapter on book tours, it goes without saying that a tour remains an extraordinary marketing undertaking.

It takes a significant amount of logistical planning and dedication: a tour is another promise made to readers and potential readers. The author is making a promise to make an appearance, or to conduct a live feed, to explore scene locations, or hold readings, or to execute many other ways that an author can employ on tour.

The marketing build-down period is what the author chooses to make of it. It depends on how intense of a commitment he or she is willing to undertake. It's a gradual transition process of marketing the new book post release, which leads towards going back into the studio to work on a new project, and will prepare readers for one's new creative era.

For indie authors, the build-down is a far greater time period than for well-established authors published from large New York publishers. The deep pockets of the big houses enable worldwide blasts of a title that lasts weeks rather than months. Typically a best seller is created, and then the houses move on to the next big title.

Because indies work with smaller budgets, we have to supplement it with the greatest and most precious resource that we have.

Time.

# THREE

**I MUST SPEND MY TIME WISELY WHILE
CREATING THE NEXT PROJECT**

I CANNOT STRESS this enough.

I made this mistake in my writing career infancy, and, as we all know, hindsight is 20/20. You might be thinking…what the heck? I need to master my craft! How can I do that without practice?

True, I agree with you.

I share your goal of becoming a master of the craft. And we are the future masters who will be educating those who will start the journey well after us. But for now, we must focus on making the general public aware of our work. Brand awareness is extraordinarily important, otherwise a sale may scarcely be made. And connection that precedes awareness is equally crucial to the ultimate sale.

If we continue the "throwing mud at the wall" method of becoming a master of the craft, and if becoming a master is the goal, we very well may reach it. But few would know about it. Because writing book after book after book, and releasing the titles into the market in a factory style, with fingers crossed and the hopes that the next book *will be the one* is a passive way to pursue one's dream. And that method is a literal shot in the dark.

We have to *make* our dreams come true.

But first, here is what I did right.

The first several novels I wrote in my career I wrote back to back to back, and when I look back on my release history, my debut novel *Ashes*, had a strong debut because I employed the "gradual build-up" marketing style prior to release.

I was talking about the novel incessantly while I was preparing it. I wasn't even aware of any "marketing style" in those days…I just was excited about my novel that I was preparing for print, and was telling everyone about it.

Things got to a point where another author friend told me, "Stop talking about it! Just release the damn thing already!" But I had to clear the creative hurdle, and while doing that, many potential readers were then aware of a new author A.L. Mengel who was about to arrive on the market in early 2013.

Now for what I did wrong.

After *Ashes* headed into print, I basked in the glory of the reviews flowing in, I was a published author! I know many of you can relate to that high; the euphoria of creating something that can be held, that can sit on a shelf, and that may still exist fifty or even one hundred years in the future. It really is quite surreal. It's the feeling I get each time when the box arrives at the door for any of my published works. It doesn't go away. Each book I hold in my hand is like a child; I celebrate their publication "birthdays" by holding promotions and giveaways, because books are special.

They are achievements.

They are works of art.

I became addicted to that euphoria. At least for a few years. And it's quite easy to fall down that funnel. When *Ashes* headed into print, like I was saying, I was riding the wave, and everything in my mind and my soul said to work on the follow up novel, *The Quest for Immortality*.

And so I got to work.

*Ashes* did well and found a readership because I employed the "gradual build-up" marketing technique without even realizing it. It never got to the "gradual build-down", because I was busy writing the next novel. I still wonder, to this day, if my debut could have had an even stronger release and market penetration had I even known about "gradual build-down" then.

But at that point, I had little willpower and was addicted to the craft.

Don't get me wrong – I love writing and I love the crafts of creative art, making music, and storytelling.

But I am also a firm believer that to gain brand awareness, readers, listeners, and to make sales from the hard work, there comes a certain point when the artist needs to become the promoter. And that is something I know now.

And so I have slowed my output down somewhat.

I still am creatively busy, but I have learned to balance my time. I know now that I have ten books of which to promote and earn sales; but I also know that I have to make a connection with my followers, earn their trust, and their loyalty, and their readership.

### *Focus on being the first*

After *Ashes* headed into print, after I felt my heart pound in my chest as I saw the partials uploading, and after I saw reviews come in, I knew I wanted to get working on my follow up novel, *The Quest for Immortality*. *Ashes* had a decent debut, I had introduced readers to the main protagonist, Antoine, and it seemed like things were going well.

I knew with just one novel, I was not ready for a tour yet, and thought that it would be good to start on the sequel. I had the story and characters fresh in my mind, and it made sense to me. *Ashes* never got a "gradual build down", but that's okay.

I started *The Quest for Immortality*, found my designer a few months later in early 2014. She is the one who, as

I mentioned earlier, I still use exclusively for covers to this day. We released some teaser artwork and set a release date of October 28, 2014.

I chose that date for a specific reason.

In my distant past, I had a conversation with a loved one. "I want to be the next Stephen King," I said. "I want to be the next Anne Rice."

He looked perplexed. "Why would you want to be the next of anything? Wouldn't you want to be the first of something?"

"Sure, but no one knows me yet."

He scoffed. "Of *course* no one knows you! You're just getting started! Give it some time. Give it some patience. Give it some effort. It will come for you, I have confidence. But you have to put in the work. The time…and the effort. It's not just going to come to you."

I nodded.

"Focus on being the first A.L. Mengel."

And then those words pierced my mind.

While I had read a multitude of Stephen King's books, and had emailed back and forth with Anne Rice in 2007 about how to get published, there I was, several years later, still wondering how I could penetrate the market.

But I chose the release date for *The Quest for Immortality* for a specific reason. I learned of Anne Rice's novel *Prince Lestat,* which she had been promoting for a while at that point. And when I look at Anne Rice's brand, I saw her loyal page followers that she calls the "People of the Page", and I saw her engagement and connection.

I knew by then that I didn't want to be the next Anne Rice. But I like to study the greats, and the greats, as well as the other A-list authors who are published by large New York houses also typically are where they are at because the processes that they employ work.

I didn't know then what was a good time to release a novel, but I now see that there are clear times when books are released, varying by the genre and time of year. When I noticed that Rice and I write about similar topics, I thought it would be prudent to release a similarly themed book on the same day.

In the subsequent years, I got away from pairing my book with the release of a mainstream author. I don't really know if releasing *The Quest for Immortality* on the same day as *Prince Lestat* hurt me or helped me, for during that time, I was still so new, and just getting my second book out to the reading public, with far less distribution, that I don't believe that it really mattered one way or another.

But still, with releasing, I gathered my own identity and style, which was important to achieve what I had been told: "Be the first A.L. Mengel."

And so I committed to the gradual build-up marketing philosophy, and, the following year, I joined a multitude of writer's groups on social media, and started connecting with other authors and making friends.

I had found the key, but still needed to locate the door.

### Brand Influencers

Conversations like the one on the previous pages had a great impact on how the A.L. Mengel brand developed over time. Whereas I didn't know, in the months leading up to the release of *Ashes*, how my brand identity would develop over the years, I had to learn the concept of branding, and a team of people helped me understand what my brand was.

My brand is me.

I repeat this point several times, because if that is the only take away from this book, then it is the most important part of the message.

Branding is quite important for a start-up artist.

In the beginning, however, I started understanding the brand concept more clearly once I formed the relationship with my designer, which I discussed in the earlier pages of this book.

While art plays a crucial role in branding, I became a better established presence on social media (particularly Facebook) through advertising. One of the biggest aspects of my brand was developed through page promotions.

I set up paid promotions inviting people to my page, which I called "The Writing Studio" from day one, all the way back in 2012.

Once I gained a better understanding of what I had to offer in terms of a product, I started thinking about something memorable – similar to a motto, or tagline – for the brand. One of the first mottos I produced was simple: "Sophisticated Horror."

Over time, I learned that I really only had one book that could be classified as "horror" (*Ashes*) and the rest were supernatural thrillers. (I had not yet ventured into science fiction at that time.)

I decided that I needed something that was more encompassing to invite people to "join" The Writing Studio. Also, I noticed how many other authors were doing the exact same thing that I was doing: publishing books, studying branding, and trying to build their base via social media.

I was one of many.

I wanted to stand out; I wanted people to remember me when they ventured to my Facebook page. Something that would "cement" in their minds and (hopefully) sell some books. I already had a website at the time, almengel.com. It was easy to remember and to tell people in a hurry. But I was thinking about my Facebook page, aka "The Writing Studio".

It wasn't until early 2016, when I was writing *War Angel*, that I had taken part in a 80's themed costume party. I went all out – the tight rolled up jeans, multi colored jelly bracelets, neon gloves – I was the quintessential 80's rock and roller. But what became the catalyst for my brand identity wasn't the 80's costume, it was the green rocker wig that I wore to complete it.

It was a bright, vivid green; the hair was a mess in all different directions, but it screamed 80's punk rock. And that is when the light bulb brightened within my mind. I had already been a concert fan, studying the music business for years, and I was well aware of pop stars who would perform and post photos to social media in vibrant costumes.

I thought to myself, could an author do something so bold? Especially an independently published author who was still on a quest for readership?

And then the conversation that I'd had years prior popped back into my mind. "Be the first A.L. Mengel."

Those words of advice had remained with me over the years, and those words cemented my decision.

I had to dress in costume.

# FOUR

## I MUST TO SPEND MONEY TO MAKE MONEY

THIS IS AN OLD business cliché. And a cliché is what it is for a reason.

It works.

If a cliché occurs in fiction, its considered overused.

But the cliché works.

And that's why many authors emulate a specific series of events or characters that are known to hook the audience. There's on old saying in news that goes *if it bleeds, it leads* and it also can be considered a storytelling cliché, for a cliché novel opening is some sort of a death, murder, etc.

But readers like those types of beginnings to hook them into a story, and urge them to read on to find out what led up to the bloody first scene.

And so it works.

And we all must learn the ultimate *marketing* cliché of the necessity to spend money to make money. While our pockets may not be as deep as the big-name A-listers, the same philosophies ring true. If we want readers to read our books, they have to be aware that our books even *exist* and we must hook them into our own excitement: potential readers must get excited about the coming story also!

So how can a reader become passionate for the project before a book is even released?

Looking back to the video that I released in early 2018, telling the story of how my Aunt had passed away unexpectedly, was a significant clue in my marketing journey. Little did I know then that I was already making a connection with my page followers, which hovered around 5,000-6,000 at that time.

While I had already built a significant base on my Facebook page in early 2018, I had little understanding of what their preferences truly were.

Or where my followers were located.

What I knew then was that my brand was already global, but I still had quite a lot to learn about those precious likes on my Facebook page.

I met with author Jeremy Croston who wrote **The Negative Man** and **Drakovia** series among other titles. We held several lunch meetings in late summer of 2017, while I was still writing *The Mortician*, and we discussed strategic marketing for our novels.

We had been meeting about monthly for several months at that point, since we both lived in the same metro area. We had our own little "writer's group" per se. However, we were both seasoned writers and published authors at that point, we both have our own brand identities, and rather than coach each other on the art of writing, which would have been completely unproductive, we opted to strategize our marketing.

No more random promotions.

No more throwing mud at the wall in the form of writing more books, in order to see what sticks and grabs the attention of the readers.

And so my writing process slowed down considerably.

While my peers were releasing several books in a single year, I headed in a completely different direction. I said to myself, "there is no way that I am going to get my books to readers if I am overwhelming them with release after release after release." And so at that time, I committed to a single book a year, and 2018 saw no writing release from me at all.

But there was the tour.

In March of 2018, while on a break after the first leg of the tour, I met with fantasy novelist C.L. Schneider at a posh convention hotel in Orlando, Florida. While we were talking shop at a small table by the pool, I expressed disdain that I was on a scheduled two-month tour break to work on *Colonia*, and that I hadn't been getting much writing accomplished at all. "I need to have a release," I told her. "I'm frustrated that I am not getting any writing done."

Her face shifted. "But you're touring!"

I nodded, and knew it was true. I had thought about what some others, who aren't even writers, had advised me on earlier that same month: they told me to focus on promotion for a while, to focus on earning a readership. Up until those conversations, I had mostly been spending all of my allotted creative time writing book after book.

And those conversations told me that 2018 was a year to promote.

### *Remove the box*

While Jeremy and I were meeting in 2017, we started discussing a tour, and how we might execute an elaborate marketing plan for indie authors with practically no budget to allocate. We sat with our books at a local Bahama Breeze and asked the server to take promotional photos of us with our books. Both *Malice of the Cross* and *The Mortician* were preparing to release on the same day, and we decided a promo photo together was in order.

When the topic turned to the tour, we both knew that we had to think creatively, and execute a tour in an unorthodox fashion. My astrological sign is Aries, and I've always thought that Aries people are usually big-picture thinkers. Before I became an author, I was a department head in various hotel and restaurant management companies. I excel at dreaming big, and in the case of the tour, I was no different. The tour had to be big. It had to be long-running, and we had to do it in a unique and exciting way.

Jeremy agreed with me 100%, but he was an important part of the equation to keep things grounded. At that point, he was already seasoned with arranging signing events whereas I had never appeared publicly as A.L. Mengel at that point. In planning the tour, we balanced each other well, and Jeremy's partnership for the first leg of the tour really helped me launch.

When we sat at Bahama Breeze and discussed the details of how we wanted to execute the tour, and when we planned to schedule events, I had the big dreams, and Jeremy was the backbone. Whereas some people have told me to "get my head out of the clouds", Jeremy recognized that I needed my head there. When I am standing in the middle of the country, in order to see the big picture, I need to see New York and San Francisco at the same time.

But I get the big picture.

And I knew that the tour had to be big, despite our monetary limitations. We weren't rock stars to the world, but our readerships thought we were rock stars. And Jeremy and I agreed that we needed to show our readers – wherever they were located – that we could set an example of how to tour on a limited budget. And create content that could be interesting.

We both knew that we needed to get out from behind the keyboard in order to make a true connection with people and earn their readership.

### Facebook is your friend

It's a running joke in my inner circles about my Facebook bill. People tell me, "Facebook is free! Why do you have to pay?"

I then explain to them that I am an advertiser, and that in order to keep Facebook free for the majority of users, there are a smaller percentage of page owners which promote posts not only to sell a product, but sometimes just for visibility. But Facebook is an extraordinary tool to make a connection if used properly. I'm not talking about randomly promoting posts (although sometimes random *can* work...but savvy marketers will go with their gut feelings, and sometimes it can be a shot in the dark, but there have been some wonderfully successful random promotions.)

But before discussions of a tour, I had adopted the cliché of needing to spend money to make money. By early 2018, I was already well-versed in the mysteriousness of Facebook advertising.

A creative should study some of the other successful pages before selecting posts for promotion. Using the example of an author once again, it is fairly easy to tell, on some pages, which posts have been promoted and which have not. I won't use a page such as Anne Rice's as an example, as I suspect, due to her following of 1.1 million. The page shows the engagement is healthy on every post. But then, Rice herself engages with followers on her page on an ongoing basis.

I've seen other pages with tens of thousands of followers where most posts are essentially ignored, or only have a handful of likes. For the amount of followers, the miniscule engagement is head scratching. However, on those same pages, there sometimes tend to be an occasional post with an extraordinary amount of engagement: perhaps several thousands likes, and also perhaps some commenting and sharing. It's when posts stand out like that where it becomes apparent that it's a promoted post.

The creative must make a decision on whether to promote *all* posts, or just select posts. If all posts are promoted, there will be engagement, depending on the budget and content. A simple act of "boosting" a post with $1 for 24 hours will gain some participation on the post, even if just a little. Therefore, when more significant posts, such as a book trailer or buy link, receives a more significant budget over a longer length of time, those bigger promoted posts won't "stick out" in a sea of posts with zero or near-zero engagement.

Why do I pay for my engagement?

Because at this stage of the game, we have to. Facebook is a business, and just like any other business, they need to make money in order to stay in operation. Facebook made the commitment that they always want to be a free service to their regular users.

But we aren't regular Facebook users.

We are in a business. Even if there are some if your life who insist that your art is a "hobby", if you are making money with it, regardless of how small the numbers are, if you create something, and you receive payment for it to be experienced by someone, you are a *business*.

And businesses need to spend money to make money, plain and simple.

## *Facebook advertising 101*

Navigating the Facebook advertising section can be seen as daunting and overwhelming at first, but starting slow and small is key. When enabling the page to create ads, a credit card, PayPal account or another payment arrangement will be required. Please keep in mind that the method of payment will be charged at the end of each calendar month, therefore it is important for the creative to keep a few things in mind.

First, as Facebook will require that a budgetary threshold be set, the creative must keep in mind they must set a limit for spending which can be comfortably afforded. Once the threshold is reached, the payment method will automatically be charged, regardless of the time of month. If the limit is not reached within a 30 day period, then the method of payment is automatically charged for the balance. After the balance is reset to zero, the process begins once again, and will continue for any long-running ads. When you set the monthly limit, remember this is a bill that you will be charged for each month. And if you exceed your budget by double, then, guess what: you are charged double.

Facebook does not let an advertiser carry a balance beyond 30 days, and all advertising will be frozen until the balance is zeroed out. I learned that lesson the hard way when my credit card had been replaced by the bank and I forgot to navigate to the advertising dashboard and update my form of payment.

That, in turn, created a problem come the end of the month when Facebook attempted to charge my card to settle my account and the charge was rejected. While I held the new card in my wallet, the old card with the old expiration date was linked to my account.

Facebook sent me a notification saying that they were unable to charge my method of payment and all of my ads were pulled and paused. The notification clearly lists the balance, so it's important to select a form of payment which can comfortably accommodate that balance, as once the data on the form of payment is entered, it is automatically charged.

It's of great importance to start with a lower budget threshold, perhaps just $25, while the new user is getting used to the layout and workings of the dashboard. I'm just sticking to the basics here, as we all know that Facebook changes on occasion for its social users, it also sometimes changes for their business users as well.

The dashboard overall is easy to navigate once one has gained a level of comfort, and that does take some time and use. That's why I recommend starting with a smaller budget, less than you can comfortably afford, at least for a short period, until you are secure enough with the dashboard and its necessity for regular monitoring.

It's quite easy, especially in the beginning, to lose track of boosted posts. If you choose to boost all page posts with a small budget and short window, each boosted post will be listed in date order on the dashboard. Selecting a small budget, of $1, will ensure that it's visible to the page followers and receives some engagement. It will also appear on news feeds of Facebook users who follow pages similar to yours.

The reach, however, increases with budget, naturally. When taking an approach of boosting all posts, I don't recommend a budget higher than the $1-$3 range, as, depending on posting frequency, it can add up quickly and get easily out of control. Daily boosted posting can eat up, and exceed, an entire month's budget without even allowing for more significant posting with larger budgets and buy links.

If a creative chooses to set a spending limit threshold of $100 each month, once the limit is reached, Facebook will automatically charge the method of payment and the ads will resume and begin charging the advertising account again. If all posts are boosted with a small budget, and if posting frequency is daily with 24 hour runs and a $3 budget, if all ads run their lifetime then $21 per week is spent of the budget, which adds to $84 at months end for a single daily boosted post. That does not allow much space in the budget for the bigger ads that lead to sales.

The bigger ads are where the focus needs to be, as the bigger ads have the potential to lead to direct sales. It's an important rule of thumb to keep the ads simple, with a hook and a direct buy link, and a budget of at least $10 and a run time of at least 10 days. This will allow time for the ad to appear in followers' news feeds more than once, allowing those people to "mull over" the purchase, and permits time for the followers to transform into readers.

Which is what followers all need to become.

# PART TWO:

# THE HOW
# STATEMENTS

# FIVE

## HOW I CAN MAKE A STRONGER CONNECTION

THIS BOOK THUS FAR has been a specific manual on what I had to do to better relate to my followers, increase my engagement, and connect, therefore, having a greater potential of turning those followers into readers. It's all a lot of interesting theory, but without the "how", then the theory becomes baseless.

There has to be a process.

There has to be a proven way to succeed in the sea of speculation and treacherous waters of assumptions: if I don't know my audiences' preferences, then how will I connect with them?

If I don't learn their location, will my advertising reach them?

And that is where the how has entered into my own marketing regime; for in order for it to be effective, marketing must be strategic and targeted. I've been repeating this point throughout the book because I believe it to be one of the most important. In the previous chapters, some examples were provided of marketing promotions that were tied into world events: Easter and Passover, the arrival of the NASA satellite Juno in the Jovian system, among others.

But there are many more.

For the savvy marketer, or the experienced book promoter, who has a penchant for being well-informed, and a talent for identifying what topics the public (and, potentially, the *reading* public) might be interested in, can be somewhat of an illusion for the indie artist.

It's as if the successful promoter is a mirage in a vast, dry, hot searing desert. The indie artist is fully and well aware that in order to connect their art with the world, there has to be promotion. Yet there are countless artists out there in the world that remain stuck, wandering the desert, desperate for a drink of water. They look at the mirage in the distance; they see the vision of flowing fresh, cold water, brilliant green tropical trees and shade, but when they approach…the vision vanishes.

Where are the followers? Where is the drink?

All they see is a dry, vast, hot desert, and feel their parched, dry mouth, wondering what happened.

But there is a way to find the mirage.

For the followers are out there.

There are readers who crave the next Anne Rice, the next Stephen King. And there are music lovers out there that would fall in love with your amazing songs…if only they knew the songs existed.

There is one important caveat, however.

One must hold an understanding of personal preferences – but not in a general sense. There are so many people across the world who are in varying demographics; and it's the demographics that a savvy marketer must understand and appreciate. Throwing mud at the wall, like we'd discussed in the previous section, does not make an effective marketing tactic.

Do you remember when I had mentioned in the previous section about doing a live feed in January of 2018 just before the *#TakeAJourney2018* book tour had kicked off? I mentioned that the live feed had become a marketing clue for me. I didn't realize it at the time, but I was just starting to gain an understanding of the preferences of the demographics on my Facebook page.

### *Gain an understanding from those who LOVE what you do*

There are those of us who have a support network, and others who don't. That's the reality of being an artist. We don't punch timeclocks and earn regular paychecks like many do; we take risks over security; we place passion in our art and need to be our own biggest cheerleaders.

But that doesn't negate the need for a support network. And if you feel that you weren't gifted one naturally, it's time to build one.

Because it's needed for the long journey.

Building a creative career is similar to building a skyscraper…laying one brick at a time.

And the thought of the brick needs to be what it truly is. The thought of bricklaying is rather simple; place the cement, add the brick. Maybe hundreds of bricks could be laid by one person in a single day.

But when comparing bricks to a creative accomplishment, it is quite different.

For the brick, if compared to an achievement for a creative, demands many more steps to lay a single brick. If a brick could be likened to gaining followers, a new reader or a reading at a library…then it would take an indie artist much more time to lay a single brick in their creative career.

This is not meant to be discouraging.

We, as indies, have a far smaller supply of the cement, to attach the bricks to our skyscraper. For if the cement is the marketing budget, we have to work with a far thinner adhesive agent.

But it can stick.

And our support networks are what make the cement stick, whether we are lucky enough to have those in our lives who naturally see the talent we have, or if we have to go out into the world, and meet people, and make contacts, and build our own support networks. For they are the glue which will hold your career together during the tough times.

But this leaves two very significant questions: how can an artist build their own support network? And how can an artist gain an understanding from them to keep adding the layers of bricks to the skyscraper?

## *On or off social media?*

We've got a conundrum on our hands, haven't we?

For those of us who not fortunate enough to have a built in support network, we have to venture out into the world and find the people who believe in our own art as much as we do. And I am not going to give any sugar coated responses here. It takes work, and it takes time.

I'm afraid that my message here can't be any clearer: the bricks will be laid at a much slower pace during this time.

It's important to have a professionally designed website as the base of operations for your brand. The site can be simple, but it needs to be clean and have some self-updating capacity and be linked to social media. On my website, almengel.com, there is a tab called The Writing Studio which is a real time feed of my Facebook page.

I rarely visit my website, but my books can be purchased from the site; a simple click on the cover will open the Amazon listing. Although its unlikely that Facebook will be disappearing anytime soon, a smart marketer will not put all of the eggs all in one basket.

When meeting people professionally, it's important to have a website, which gives added credibility to the brand. If a brand is completely reliant on Facebook and other forms of social media, there *can* be the perception of it being "less serious", regardless of the actuality of the creative behind the brand.

## *The support network*

There is a big wide world of potential readers, listeners and consumers *beyond* the social media world. There are many who choose not to participate in the social media world. But the money that they bring to your brand is just as significant and necessary for success as the money that rolls in from social media supporters.

The support network, on the other hand, is a critical component of success.

This is the section where I will contradict myself (somewhat) and regarding what I said in a previous section about family. If family and friends are supportive of your venture, they can be some of your biggest cheerleaders. If your creative venture is well respected by your friends and family, half of your battle has already been won. There are those in your life already who may be telling their friends that they know an author, and that they love your books or your music, and that can spread in networks and help with word of mouth advertising. Never be afraid to give copies of your work to friends and family.

Don't always expect a review.

But you might get a read.

And if you don't, the book might still get passed on to someone who *will* read it and possibly review the book. And even if the book gets read and still isn't reviewed, the word may still be spread a little about your book, and word of mouth advertising is worth its weight in gold, and the value of the marketing far exceeds the cost of one book.

# SIX

**HOW I CAN TOUR LIKE A ROCK STAR**

DOES THE IDEA OF A BOOK TOUR sound daunting to you?

It did to me, at least for a while. I saw other indie authors conduct "blog tours", which I never really fully understood. I think it was when a blogger would feature that author and their work on their blog for a post, and then the author would move to another blog, and keep touring the blogs until they got tired of it. I suppose it might have been effective for some, but I honestly couldn't understand how that type of marketing plan would work for me.

Or anyone, for that matter.

At that point in my life, when I was starting to think about getting out from behind the keyboard and getting in front of the people, I didn't understand how sending an email with some book cover photos, a bio and some canned interview questions and answers would help my brand at all.

I knew then that I wanted to be different, and have a new way of marketing for an indie author. And so I started thinking about touring.

I went to a bunch of concerts.

I started to study the music business.

And this is the point where start up musicians and bands need to pay attention.

Touring like a rock star seems out of reach for many, but it really isn't. Sure, a rock band style tour, with packed arenas and stadiums, driving between cities in a posh tour bus, or, even better, in a fancy private jet with stays in luxurious hotel suites, seems unreachable for many.

As it should.

It's the rock star lifestyle.

And it's afforded to few.

But I thought that there just had to be a way that an indie author could tour like a rock star – maybe not with the big crowds in bookstores in every city – but I believed there just *had* to be a way that an indie could make an impact on their own career with a small budget.

And so that is when I called Jeremy Croston, and we met to start planning the tour.

He was as excited as I was, and during one of our meetups, we declared the tour official. We knew that we would start the tour small, in Central Florida, because Jeremy had contacts throughout that area.

I did not.

My brand was already global, but I wasn't selling enough to justify a world tour. Actually, I *still* am not selling enough yet to justify a world tour, but I am still planning one. When Jeremy and I met, we started strategizing, and put our heads together to figure out how we could tour as authors. I had explained to him how I had been going to concerts and studying the music business, and how music artists tour.

We knew that we were not at the stage of our careers when Barnes and Noble book signings would have crowds and a line around the block with eager readers taking photos and getting books signed. A great goal to have, but the reality is that many indie authors won't command a crowd of that magnitude at a signing or reading.

I also knew at that time, that a large percentage of my readers were overseas, and should I have a book signing at Barnes and Noble, I would probably have spent a great deal of time sitting at the table and having conversations with the staff. I didn't really see that approach as a viable option for a start-up indie preparing a tour.

Jeremy, however, did have a local following which he said could help me. And that is one of the reasons why we complemented each other well for a book tour: he wanted to expand his brand on a global scale, and I wanted to gain some local readers. So it was a good match. He had the contacts to arrange some local events to kick off the tour.

These were to be events where people would actually show up, people with whom we could discuss our books with face to face, and who would take an interest in our work. Jeremy arranged the opening event, and I just pretty much tagged along. He had the contacts and the readers, and it led to an exciting first event of the tour.

On the morning of the tour, I was excited. It was the first time – officially – that I would be entering the public as A.L. Mengel. I was nearly five years into my writing career at that point, still a novice in literary standards, but I knew, deep within my soul, that I needed to get out from behind the keyboard.

Jeremy was already well seasoned with appearances in the local market; I was not.

At the start of the tour, I had never had a book signing. In fact, I hadn't even really discussed my books yet with strangers "in real life". I was quite confident online, and already was considered a successful Indie in the literary community; I was recognized as the creator of *#Writestorm*, and was getting known in the Indie Author networks.

Making the move to in-person interactions was a necessary direction at that stage of my career, and I had to obtain a level of comfort and ease discussing my work with people I didn't know.

I had arrived at the shop early, and decided to grab some lunch from a restaurant down the street since the event wasn't scheduled to begin until 2pm. When I was finishing up my meal, I received a phone call from Jeremy that I will always remember.

"We have to get over there," he said.

"It's still pretty early. Why so early?"

"Because Krum's World called me to say that people have been there waiting for us since before noon!"

I grabbed my check and sprang into action.

This was it, the moment was here.

There was a group of people at a small comic shop who had already been waiting an hour to meet A.L. Mengel and Jeremy Croston.


### *Limit Overhead and Don't Focus on Selling*


I'm a firm believer in "gradual build-up" marketing and promotion leading up the release of a product. I've practiced it throughout my writing career, and, in this case, the product was the tour. I put an announcement trailer together and announced the tour on social media the day after Christmas in 2017. While Jeremy and I were still planning the tour, I was already excited, as I hadn't seen other indie authors embark on a tour of this style.

A week or so later, I saw another indie author announce a tour – with a slightly different style. It was a tour of comic cons. It was similar to my own book tour as it was long running as well, and I felt as if we were indie author "pioneers", carving out new directions for Indies, although with different styles.

In the planning of the tour, Jeremy and I had looked at Comic Cons, and made the decision that the Con route wasn't for us. We saw that it was a significant amount of overhead – booth rental and registration fees, inventory, travel and food related expenses, all without making a single sale.

I declared early on, that I didn't want to feel pressured on the tour; I wanted to be able to be relaxed and had confidence that the sales would come as a result of a no-pressure, no-selling tour. I just wanted to go out, meet the people, connect with them, and tell them about my work.

Jeremy loved this idea, and without the pressure of sales, we were allowed to have *fun* and be ourselves, and to me, that is what the tour was all about. It turned out that the tour *was* a success – from the very beginning. It provided me with a very important clue.

Do you remember when I said I went on live video with Jeremy in early 2018 while planning the tour? It was an important clue as to the preferences of my social media followers. I learned, over the following years, that my followers like to see me on video. I don't know if they like the sound of my voice, or if I sound like a person that is genuine, or that they find me nice to look at or listen to. Or perhaps a combination of all of them. But it was two live feeds that I did with Jeremy in January of 2018, while planning the tour, that birthed my direction into video.

### Aces in their places

I was fortunate enough to work at two television studios while in school, and while I didn't know it at the time, it was preparing me for what I have been doing currently. During the period in school, I learned a lot of editing, video production, set design, camera angles and more. In college, I worked at the campus video production studio, and I had the rather boring job of recording guest lectures, and then editing them into a final video for the university.

Fast forward a number of years, and it was just after the release of *The Mortician.*

I had already released a series of trailers for that title, as I had become quite aware that I really enjoyed video production, and I was quite happy with the results. But live video is a different animal altogether.

I had been experimenting with live feeds since late 2016, so I had become more comfortable, over time, in front of a live camera, regardless of the size of the audience. I will always remember the first time I went live on Facebook, from my personal profile on December 20, 2016. At that time, I had started to get known as the author who was into cosplay, dressing as a character in costume, and I embraced that analysis.

Regardless of what my followers and peers thought in 2016, I knew, in my own mind, that my costumes had a specific purpose: my costumes were always a vision of my characters, or inspiration of characters that I had created. I knew that people generally would not recognize them at the time, but I felt that once my stories gained notoriety, and mainstream attention, that some of the references might seem obvious.

When I went live on my personal page, I was in character costume, and it was the same costume I had been wearing in my profile photo at the time. I duplicated it to the last detail, and decided I had to try this whole "going live" trend which was happening. My heart started pounding in my chest as I saw the big red button. And I honestly thought my voice was shaking the entire time, but upon playback, it didn't seem noticeable.

"I am coming to you live…as my profile photo."

That is what I had said. But little did I know, in 2016, that it was one of the original live feeds which I would naturally gravitate towards.

Fast forward to 2018.

I was scheduled to meet up with Jeremy to plan a book tour stop in Winter Park, Florida, and we both knew that a live feed had been part of the tour planning stop. There was some uncertainty, however, in how to execute the video. The Winter Park stop had been decided upon as there was a small, independent bookshop in a picturesque area which we both thought would be a great bookshop to possibly hold a signing.

The interesting thing was not the bookshop – it actually didn't make it on the final tour due to consignment issues. What became memorable about Winter Park was the live feed. "Let me read from *Malice of the Cross*," I offered, and Jeremy agreed. We started the video together, with a very spontaneous feel. The camera was shaking, and in the beginning, I think my voice was a bit as well. There's something about going live – especially on a public page. At that point, the A.L. Mengel page already had a few thousand followers, and when I pressed that big red button, I knew there was a chance that strangers from across the world would be watching us. But then, that was the point, and when I handed off the phone to Jeremy, I had no idea if we had anyone watching.

I read from Jeremy's book and then took the camera back, and we walked to the bookstore on live video.

I will always remember this video fondly, because it was the first time that Jeremy and I went live together, on a tour planning stop for the #TakeAJourney2018 book tour.

Later that same afternoon, Jeremy and I stopped for lunch after speaking with the staff at the small book shop. I was surprised to see that the video had already received several hundred views on social media.

I immediately called Jeremy and setup a Facebook promotion, as we were both elated that people were actually watching the live feed in the middle of a weekday afternoon.

Several weeks later, we had another tour planning stop at 'Gods and Monsters', a combination comic book shop and bar in the shadow of Volcano Bay Water Park at Universal Orlando. Jeremy and I stopped by the shop together, as the shop owners had already expressed an interest in hosting our book signing. Jeremy and I agreed that we absolutely had to go live in 'Gods and Monsters', because the setting was absolutely fabulous. It was a first class comic book shop. Not only did it have beautiful, shiny hardwood floors, gigantic comic heroes everywhere, and life size stormtroopers, but, in the back, there was a bar dressed in the macabre.

It was perfect for our book signing...and even more perfect for a live feed.

The staff at 'Gods and Monsters' was very hospitable, and when they learned that we wanted to conduct a live feed in their store, they all cleared into the back for us to have a meeting and let us use their entire store for our live video promotion.

That weekend was a holiday weekend, and, from the success of the first live feed in Winter Park a few weeks prior, we both agreed that the live feed needed to be promoted.

But what was fascinating about this live video that would be destined to be a historic part of the A.L. Mengel page, the Jeremy Croston page, and the #TakeAJourney2018 Book Tour, was that, simply due to the business pairing with 'Gods and Monsters', the check-in, and promotion, led to our most viewed feed by live-viewers, and nearly seven thousand views from the three-day promotion.

Jeremy and I were ecstatic.

The world knew about our tour. And with the first event just a few short weeks away, that was a good, and somewhat nerve wracking feeling: it was starting to happen, whether we liked it or not.

### *The tour becomes the connection*

In the previous sections, the first event of the Book Tour was described in detail, so I'm not going to repeat myself here. But *beyond* that first unforgettable event is where this section will begin. Because as a reader of this book, it might seem surreal to read about authors who have multiple published novels, an increasingly established social media presence, and connections in the industry to arrange book signings.

So what is a startup to do to get their book, art, music or product into the hands of consumers? And how can one who is just starting out execute something so glamorous as a tour?

After the 'Gods and Monsters' book signing stop in late February 2018, that was the precise question that I had myself.

Because in those days, I knew that Jeremy would only be able to tour with me on the first leg. When we planned things out the previous year, there had been some discussion about expanding the tour beyond Central Florida, but I knew that Jeremy would only be able to participate in the first leg, locally.

Once the 'Gods and Monsters' book signing took place, there was a certain plateau that slowly developed. The first leg was over, we were about to start a two month break, and Jeremy's participation was pretty much over, except for two aspects: #BookOnABench and the #AuthorDiscussionSeries.

Those two hashtags helped with marketing the tour, not only to readers, but also to fellow writers. Jeremy Croston and I were in agreement that we wanted to make this tour beneficial to other writers, at least in the local area. In the #AuthorDiscussionSeries, we decided to explore topics that would affect not only writers in the Central Florida area, but writers worldwide. And especially from the perspective of an author who is independently published.

But before we cover this topic, there needs to be some explanation and connection with those who are reading this book who are *not* authors.

I've been going on and on about making a connection, and how connections can lead to sales, and for the most part, I have been speaking from an author's perspective.

But I want to make sure that the other creatives who may be reading this book are not left out. And all of you never will be left out! This book is for *all* start-ups because we all have products.

We all, ultimately, want to attract consumers and generate sales.

So for those of you who are *not* authors, now is the time for you to listen carefully. Because being an independently published Author is a double edged sword.

Finally, we can say that our work is in print.

Most likely it will live longer than we do.

But getting the writing out to the general public, and I am talking about *beyond* family and friends, is where the challenge comes in. And for those of you who are artists or musicians, or even entrepreneurs, you are all quite well aware of the challenges surrounding a start-up. And the idea of a tour, creating content in a live setting which can filter to online followers, can be a very effective marketing tool, with ongoing event promotion and boosting.

***Embrace family. But still keep them at a distance.***

People want to support you.

But they also want to support success.

That is where the hurdle is placed.

And it's a big one.

Because, most likely, there are other members of your own family who have scaled that hurdle decades ago in their own disciplines, and when you approach them with your amazing and wonderful idea, they might scoff at it. There will always be others who did something similar, decades ago. Despite that, there will always be that one member of the family who encourages your progress. It may be one, or it may be several, or even quite a few family members.

But as you project a seriousness about your work, members of your family, whom you might have thought to be roadblocks, will step up and take you and your work more seriously. Even if the royalties aren't yet flooding your bank accounts with cash, behave as if they are. Use the words, "I have to work," and then sit down and write. Professional writing is sometimes seen as a hobby, because it doesn't bring a regular paycheck. But associating the writing with the word "work" can gradually change perception. Always respect your work time. When people walk by you, don't be spending time on YouTube watching videos or Facebook chatting with friends. Because when people see that, the credibility of the writing job is diminished.

When you say, "I have to work," the manuscript should be open. Notetaking, character building and more, can always take place on the side in a notebook. Respect given to the job of writing can earn it from others who might perceive it as a hobby.

The working writer produces a book. The working artist produces a painting or a sculpture. The working singer produces an album. The working entrepreneur produces a product or business plan. Show your loved ones that this truly is respected work, and they will come to respect it as well, even if there isn't a regular paycheck involved.

I experienced something similar to this on my own when I was preparing *Ashes* for publication.

During family gatherings, I was always telling everyone how I wanted to be an author, how my novel was always almost ready, but somehow, never fully ready. Everyone in my family was fully supportive in those days years ago, but in my heart, I knew that I wanted to show them all that I was taking this new direction seriously. And that *Ashes* was not some one time venture: I really desired to form a true writing career.

Over the years, I learned to keep my family, who, in the beginning, were my biggest supporters, and my most welcome critics, at a distance.

My work had to have its own merits in the world.

I knew that my family could not carry me through my writing career; only my writing had that power. And that is where the uncertainty fought its way through. I had been elated to wake up to glowing Amazon reviews from family, but I knew, in order to be successful, I had to distance my work from my family and send it, truly, out into the world.

## *The uncertainty of a tour*

Leaving my family in the rearview mirror, I knew that the sky was the limit, but I didn't know if I quite measured up. Jeremy Croston and I were already on tour together, but I honestly had some doubts about myself.

I remember when the owner handed the microphone to me at 'Krum's World' just after introducing me as A.L. Mengel. Now a little background. At that point, I had yet to make an appearance publicly as A.L. Mengel. Certainly, Jeremy and I already made several live videos, where I was appearing in the video as A.L. Mengel.

But at Krum's World, things were different. Now I was truly in public, with live people sitting in an audience, waiting to hear what A.L. Mengel had to say.

Holding the microphone, I looked out in the crowd. Probably about fifty people. Jeremy was standing off to the side; it was my time to introduce myself to the Orlando reading market.

They stared back at me, and waited for me to speak.

Who is this A.L. Mengel?

And then the doubt, and the uncertainty set in.

My voice sounded strange – tinny – on the microphone. I could feel my heart thumping in my chest, and thought there might have been a slight quiver in my voice, but I probably will never know if the audience knew it or not.

There was something surreal about making the first appearance as A.L. Mengel. I had to stop myself when introducing myself – my name was not Andrew. Or Andy. It was A.L., and I was a published author. When I met people and shook their hands, I had to remember who I was. I'm A.L. Mengel. I had to get comfortable with talking about my books. And my characters. Because that is why someone would want to meet and talk with A.L. Mengel. Not to learn about my personal life, although I have been sharing more of it on my public page in bits and pieces lately. At the time, no one knew who A.L. Mengel was, but they knew that he was a special guest at the event which they were attending, and they wanted to know about my characters and books.

And so Krum's World became a precipice for me.

I was standing at the edge of a cliff; that split second that I took the microphone from the shop owner, and as I looked out towards the sea of faces, all eyes on me, and felt the thump of my heartbeat, I knew that I was in the precise moment where my writing career would truly begin.

"Hello, I am A.L. Mengel," I said to the audience.

### *Blossoming from an event into a tour*

The Krum's World kick-off event was February 10, 2018, and the Gods and Monsters signing was February 28, 2018. On February 21, Jeremy and I held an event with local authors called the #AuthorDiscussionSeries. The vision was to have discussions about pertinent topics in the publication business, in a real life format, and offered in an online alternative.

The #AuthorDiscussionSeries was a great way to create content for the tour and to connect with our online audience, especially those who would not be able to attend events. It was also something that was

easily executable for indie authors. The store events —
Krum's World and Gods and Monsters — were not as
easy to come by. We had to put in a lot of work. Make
numerous phone calls, and send many e-mails. But they
worked out.

Since we were both planning and executing the tour
ourselves, we had to keep overhead and administration
to a minimum. Our time was best served creating
content and attending events. And the
#AuthorDiscussionSeries was a great way to create
content for the tour which our online audience would
connect to, who wouldn't be able to attend the event
anyway due to distance.

The tour break was looming, and I knew that Jeremy
was going to be dropping off the tour. Plus, I was eager
to work on *Colonia* which I had outlined at that point
in a general format.

This was late February of 2018.

In early March, right around the time that I made my
massive mistake of believing that I could complete a
two-novel set, which I had scarcely started to write,
with a same-day release in Fall of 2018.

In a touring year.

As February came to a close, my confidence was through the roof. When I wasn't attending the three scheduled events for that month, I was in my studio working on *Colonia*. My biggest blunder of the year was to create a trailer promising my page followers an epic science fiction story by Fall of that year.

But during those days, I knew little of how much a tour can take over one's planning and time. Later in March, when C.L. Schneider told me that I was touring, I realized that releasing a book in 2018 didn't need to be on my list of things to do. But I still went into the studio obsessively, even if just to write a few sentences here or there, and perhaps outline something or work on a character's development.

When April came, I was increasingly dissatisfied with my word count, the tour break was almost over, and Jeremy's schedule had changed. It had become increasingly uncertain if he could participate in April's events, and after the April events, I knew I was truly on my own. It turned out that Jeremy and I met for one last #AuthorDiscussionSeries event on April 3, 2018, and then we had to part ways for a while.

So in early April, I was truly touring on my own.

When I thought about and wondered how I was going to write and finish *Colonia* for a fall release, I listened to C. L. Schneider's words reverberate through my head "but you're touring!" In my mind, the March tour break was supposed to get a good percentage of the books drafted (remember it's a two book set). But I had scarcely gotten through the openers. I knew that I couldn't write two novels in the detailed format that I had always employed in a few short weeks. It just wasn't happening.

And so I listened to C. L. and put *Colonia* away.

It was time to focus on the tour.

It was also during this time that I made a decision that was critical to the success of the remaining months of the tour. I knew that I had to focus on the tour. And keep my head in *The Mortician*, which had been my most recent release and was the showcased book for the tour. I knew, in my mind, that I needed a break from the deep subject matter of *The Mortician*, and I got that break with the creation of my science fiction epic two novel set, along with the February events of the tour.

But as May was looming, it was time to focus on the tour, and get my head back into the story of *The*

*Morticia.* I needed to get the tour, the national events, and the events beyond Florida, that I could only execute myself, underway.

And that's when the magic really started to happen.

### Make and share memories

When the first leg of the #TakeAJourney2018 Book Tour concluded and Jeremy and I shook hands and patted each other on the back for a job well done, the work was really just starting for me. But the first events of the tour with Jeremy gave me the boost – and the confidence – needed to tour on my own. When I boarded a flight to Atlantic City for the first out of state leg of the tour, rather than nervousness, I felt a deep excitement.

I couldn't wait to execute my plans and create my content to personally connect with my social media audience. After I completed the much needed task of putting *Colonia* on the back burner, I kept my thoughts in darker places, but more specifically, with the scenes and settings of my 2017 novel *The Mortician.* I chose to focus on the one title for the next leg of the tour, and that brought more focus to the tour.

## *Tour a book, not the collection*

After the events of February 2018, I learned that my table setup was "too busy" and potential readers were most likely overwhelmed with my offerings. The #TakeAJourney2018 Book Tour was never envisioned as a selling tour, Jeremy and I were very adamant about that.

Still, I opted to place copies of all of my titles on the table, which created somewhat of a chaos of books for would-be readers to come over and decide which title appealed to them. I found, in the following months, that I was more successful in focusing on one book, *The Mortician.* Had I been at a comic con selling booth, I would have absolutely set up all of my titles for sales, and more than likely would have had far more table space.

But with this type of tour, I really was introducing my brand to the world. "Oh my, you've written all of these books!" And the would-be reader becomes overwhelmed. They don't know which book is the best, which questions to ask, or even where to start.

Once I focused on *The Mortician*, I found my own direction within the tour. The leg with Jeremy was already over at that point, and I was on my own. I had started to employ an interesting concept, which I did not invent, called #BookOnABench. For those of you who are not familiar with the concept, it's when an author leaves a copy of their book on a bench or somewhere that a potential reader can discover their work.

Before the tour started, I spent time creating a brochure with tour specific artwork which would-be readers could keep as an artistic – yet promotional and informative – takeaway. On the front was a photo of me, taken in 2017 as a promotional photo for *The Mortician*. That photo carried over to the back, where all of my works were listed, as well as links to all of my social media and website.

The interior was vastly different.

It featured a photo of me in angel costume, in a 2016 photo taken for a *War Angel* promotion, which has since been used for various social issue posts. A quote from the book was placed inside next to the photo:

*He spread his wings. It was not as if there were a gigantic crash of demons falling from the Heavens; it was as if music was playing in every dimension; a chorus of angels bathed in gold and dreams realized, and love which was always understood.*

*Become a Beloved Friend today. Join #TheWritingStudio!*

I chose to feature my two best books (at least from my own perspective) in the brochure: *The Mortician* on the cover, which was the headlining book on the tour, and *War Angel,* which was considered by some, at that point, to be the best book of my career. Everything else was listed, including how to find me and my work, conveniently on the back, and it became an interesting takeaway.

When I was starting to execute #BookOnABench, I placed one of these brochures in each book, along with a note, letting the finder know that the book was theirs to keep, or to give to a friend or family member who might enjoy the story.

Each book drop was treated like an event. I conducted a live feed, letting my page followers know the approximate location of where I planned to leave the books. One of the reasons why this was important was because I'd already established a viewing audience on my page from the live feeds I'd done months previously with Jeremy Croston. And that is an important clue to what my page followers like: they like to see me on video.

Do you remember many pages ago when I mentioned that my first live feed with Jeremy was a clue? And that my video I recorded discussing the death of my aunt was also a clue?

It took me a few months to realize what was happening on my page, but my followers were telling me loud and clear through their engagement with my videos: this is what we like. And another thing that I noticed, over the years, while studying the insights that Facebook offers on the page, is not only to determine where my audience lives, but also gender, age group, and likes/dislikes.

Not every post is going to be a slam dunk.

## *Learn about your followers: video is the present*

And that's where the analytics come in to the equation. Once a page has established itself as a Facebook advertiser – by creating a budget, targeting an audience, and boosting a post – that process creates insights, which Facebook provides, under a tab in the advertising section. This identifies everything a page manager needs to know about their audience.

Each post is listed on the advertising manager page with the specific analytics: how many people viewed the post (the reach), which is how many people the post reached. The data also indicates many people liked the post, and how many people engaged with the post (commented, shared). For promoted posts with a video, there are two main numbers to focus on: the reach (how many people started watching the video) and the thru-play rate (how many people watched the video all the way to the end).

I learned from the thru-play rate that my watchers prefer shorter videos. On videos that were either short or had a topic that seemed to be of interest to my base (example: the *Colonia* pre-order trailer) had some of the highest thru-play rates (in some cases as much as 50%) of all of my promoted videos. Whereas my longer videos, the #Unmasked series, and videos where I just seemed to go on and on, the thru-play was less. Perhaps 10 or 20%.

Keeping the message short and to the point (under one minute overall) opened up some promotional doors for me. For one, the thru-play rate was higher on the shorter videos, which to me makes sense. I tried to imagine people scrolling through their news feeds and coming across my video. Most phones auto-play videos now, so they would at least see the first few seconds of my video.

If my message was intriguing enough, they would stay, just for a single minute, watch the entire video and get the message. But what about those that watch a few seconds and scroll onwards? The goal was to deliver them the message too.

It's important to keep in mind that, in shorter promotional videos, the video needs to be front loaded. The entire message must then be delivered at the start of the video. The message needs to be simple, easy to remember, and given in the first three seconds.

Anything after that is bonus for someone who wants to stay a little longer and watch the entire video. The message then must be delivered again, as a reminder, at the end of the video.

But the key is to keep things simple and hook the viewers in.

One important thing to remember is that video is the present. Social media is filled with videos that people can watch on their news feeds, and video has become a catalyst for connection. Live feeds are extraordinarily popular, especially among public figures. Video is the present, and has proven to be a very effective marketing tool which has enabled me to gain a reach of nearly a half million on Facebook promoted posts.

### *Catchy headlines deliver the message to non-watchers*

So now let's get back to the tour and *The Mortician*.

This is why catchy headlines have extreme importance.

The best headlines can deliver the message (and the hook) simply in the headline. So if the scroller doesn't stop scrolling long enough to dig deeper into the post, they've at least received the messaged if they stopped scrolling long enough to read the headline.

One such successful example of this principle is the video post that was directly attached to the #BookOnABench drop for *The Mortician* on the #TakeAJourney2018 Book Tour in May of 2018. I had learned of a "haunted house" in the attraction of Old Town in Kissimmee, Florida, and knew that they had an actual coffin in the window. I arrived the morning, when the outdoor shop and bar attraction was pretty much deserted, and was able to get some great photos which I immediately shared to my page, letting my followers know that a book drop was about to happen.

The photos served as clues as to where the book was going to be left. While most of my followers were from other shores, I had doubts in my mind that anyone who followed my page would pick up the copy of *The Mortician* that I had planned to leave next to the coffin in the window.

But the page proved me wrong.

Later that same day, I sat down in my studio and turned on my computer. I was surprised to find a photo of *The*

*Mortician*, in the hands of a zombie corpse in a coffin. It was clearly inside the attraction at Old Town where I had left the book. They posted it right on my Facebook page in all its horrifying glory. And I learned one of two things: either I already had local followers at that time, or I gained a new one…and possibly many…from the post on my page directly by the attraction.

But this tour stop wasn't over.

Because just after leaving the book, I shot a video, making it clear that the book was left right next to a coffin. And that is where the "catchy headline" comes in. One of the reasons why it is important to promote posts on Facebook, but video posts in particular, is the ability to create a headline.

The headline is where the hook and the message can reside. So if a would-be reader scrolls by your post – but still reads the headline – they've received the message.

And if the headline has a big enough hook, then the scroller might be turned into a clicker, and then a video watcher. The headline that was particularly successful was for the video taken of the book left for someone to find sitting next to the coffin. It employed both the message and the hook: *A.L. Mengel Leaves a Copy of 'The Mortician' Next to an Actual Coffin.*

While the video released on Facebook, some of the videos propelled me to develop a YouTube account. While the views on YouTube seem rather insignificant as compared to the views received on Facebook, the uploading of selected videos to the platform have had a significant marketing purpose. The above video frequently appears within the first several videos on an internet search, increasing results, and reaching a larger audience through search engines.

### *Focus on the search engines*

Over the years, people have commented on how often I search for myself on the internet. I search for myself and my work almost daily. Search Engine Optimization (SEO) is a critical component of marketing one's brand. While it can seem to the casual onlooker to be somewhat self-absorbed to search for oneself on the internet almost daily, it's just been a regular business practice for myself.

There's a process I use for SEO.

Typically, when the idea for a novel first enters my mind, it starts with a title. In the creative process I generally flesh out the story from there. One of the reasons I start with a title is to enable an internet search at the beginning of the project. There have been some titles that have had extraordinary searchability due to their uniqueness: *The Blood Decanter* and *The Arrival of Destiny* have both become easily discovered titles through internet search engines. Others have been not as easy to find, such as *Ashes* and *War Angel*, due to the commonality of those titles. Regardless, titles that aren't as easy to find, I have found, are often listed along with the titles that dominate the internet searches.

Another possibility that *The Blood Decanter* has become one of, if not the most easily searched title in my library, could be that it was entered into a contest with the Horror Writer's Association shortly after release for the Bram Stoker Award.

There are two titles which are fairly easy to find as well, *The Mortician* and *The Wandering Star*. Both of those titles were already common: there's a song called "The Wanderin' Star", as well as other published books that share the same title. As for *The Mortician*, there are numerous films that have the same title, and when it comes to a search for *The Mortician Book,* my novel appears right next to one of the world's most famous morticians, Caitlin Doughty, who has several published books about her experiences as a mortician, as well as a popular vlog on YouTube called "Ask a Mortician".

These search engine pairings weren't necessarily planned.

I read Ms. Doughty's book while conducting my own research for *The Mortician.* When I had titled *The Wandering Star,* it was merely by chance, as was *The Blood Decanter.* And it's important to mention that when using a principle of SEO for book titles, it takes a great deal of patience to see the results of a Google knowledge panel or pairing with more mainstream titles.

# SEVEN

## HOW I CAN PREVENT OVER-MARKETING

IT TOOK ME A WHILE to learn this concept. But it rings true in any venture; no matter how much one is in love with their artistic work, the general public is not. At least not quite yet. Granted, there are many adoring readers, listeners, and consumers who fall in love with a creative project or product. But it takes quite a bit of marketing to let the world know that your artistic masterpiece or brilliant new product even exists.

As a newly published author, when I was brand new to social media marketing, I understood the power of the social media platforms as an effective way to reach audiences. What I still needed to learn back in 2013 was that I couldn't keep on driving the same message to the same small group of people (buy my book, it's great!) who will grow weary of seeing the same posts over and over. It's more effective to focus on building the audience through page promotion on Facebook or Twitter, pin a post or tweet to the top, and set a low, daily advertising budget with a ceiling that can be comfortably afforded. Your Facebook and/or Twitter pages will then be visible and marketed to the general public, or to those who have been targeted by location, age range, or through interests using keywords. These page promotion ads, when built with a budget that one can safely afford if maxed, can be a "set and forget" type of ad that can either run daily for a set period of time, or ongoing with no specific ending date for the promotion.

This style of audience building can prove effective if the page is strong. Depending on which countries are on the target for the ad, there will be differences in responsiveness. There are options to build a custom audience on each Facebook ad.

Focusing on audience building and casting "a wider net" assists with two things. One, it helps distract the new marketer from making too many posts about the same thing and exhausting their friends on their personal profile, which can lead to friends "silencing" posts trying to sell a product or request reviews. In the most severe cases, those types of posts can be reported as spam, which never helps with reputation.

Image is critical for any new artist or entrepreneur who is working daily to find and connect with their audience or customers.

The second thing that casting a wider net helps with is giving the marketer something to focus on between projects. While we are all passionate about our creative projects and products, it's important to keep in mind the previous topics of "gradual build-up" and "gradual build-down" marketing. The general public needs time to discover the new book, album or product. And that doesn't happen instantly. Or over days or even weeks.

It can sometimes take months.

The savvy marketer understands that trust needs to be earned. The author might proclaim that their book is wonderful, but the real judge is the reader. Casting a wider marketing net through audience building will attract people to your page because they are interested in what your page offers. Always pin a selling post.

Always make sure that there is a buy link. But never directly sell.

The connection is an art, and it's important to study the social media pages that have achieved higher likes and reach, and particularly engagement, in order to see how they are connecting with their audience. And the savvy marketer will then research their own audience, determine location, and use the more successful pages as guidance.

### *How I determine a releasing schedule that works for my readership*

This topic will have more of an application with authors, artists and musicians. Whereas a start-up entrepreneur may have numerous products or services which they may market, in my years as a published author, I have found, at least in my own experience, that it's quite easy to do "too much too soon". I believe that this applies to musicians as well.

Authors tend to have backlists, and it's sometimes a common practice to release books in close succession.

This model may work for numerous authors, however it's not a principle that I chose to employ during my own writing and promotional journey. I have been told, over time, that a book a year is a good general rule of thumb. In addition, I have also studied and observed the standards of New York traditional publishing, as well as the releasing schedules of more mainstream authors. While some authors, like Stephen King, sometimes release two books in a single calendar year, I noticed most of them released at a more infrequent schedule.

I made the conscious decision that I wanted to average a book a year. I knew that I was too early on in my writing career to take years off; I would risk losing the audience that I had worked so hard to establish. However, I also didn't want to overwhelm them with too many releases in too short of a period.

There were three years which saw two releases: 2015, 2016 and 2017. 2018 saw no release; however I was touring during that year. And 2019 saw a double release, which I had been gradually promoting throughout 2018 and 2019: *The Arrival of Destiny* and *Battle of the Trinity,* which were two volumes of the same story and both released on the same day as two full novels. Granted, my releasing and marketing style may not work for everyone, but it has earned me a worldwide following and readership, at a slow and steady pace.

I understand the desire to become an overnight success.

I share those same dreams.

However, my path to success is laid out in stepping stones. And I always network with other peers to see how they are managing their own marketing versus their releasing schedule. It's great to see what works, and doesn't work, for others.

There's a lot of great ideas residing with our peers.

# EIGHT

## HOW I CAN COLLABORATE AND GET TO THE NEXT STEP

COLLABORATION CAN BE A WONDERFUL thing sometimes.

Jeremy Croston and I collaborated with the tour.

We haven't yet paired on writing a book together; and I know that countless authors have joined creative forces with one another, over many years. A number of them have created fantastic novels that have gone down in history as some wonderful stories with more than one author at the storytelling helm. This could be somewhat opinion based. However, I believe that a successful book writing partnership can happen when the two authors can fuse their styles together for seamless transitions between chapters.

A number of years back, I remember another author (not Jeremy) who was very interested in writing a book together with me. Back in those days, I had yet to learn the skill of managing differences in writing style versus the similarities in voice that were required for a smooth and readable story. The author went so far as to email me the first chapter, and asked that I continue the story and write the second chapter.

Our voices were drastically different, to a point that I was attempting to make my own writing voice sound like the other writer's, and despite numerous efforts, I couldn't do it.

In addition, I wasn't all that excited about the topic. I knew then that it wasn't a story that I would have written, and no matter how hard I tried to twist the plot, I decided against it, as the story that I'd already been sent would have lost its essence.

Over the years, I have viewed collaboration from a different perspective.

Jeremy is an excellent author, and I do believe that I am not too shabby myself. Our writing and storytelling styles are quite different, however, and the differences in voice can be challenging with any collaboration project. That doesn't mean that collaborations can't happen between two authors such as myself and Jeremy. But there would be a creative period in production needed to blend our writing styles together. So who knows what the future holds for myself, my brand, and book collaborations.

It certainly can be fun if executed correctly.

### *How I will break through the bubble: the rule of three*

Above, I had mentioned that I look at collaboration differently, and that is a true statement. When the idea is viewed from a marketing and promotional perspective, I set my sights high and look for other authors who I consider peers to join forces with, or even authors who are just beginning their marketing journey.

I believe that we all need to have at least one peer friend in our discipline, at least one who you aspire to become, and another who you can take under your wing and assist and guide them along their own journey.

While I wouldn't go so far as to call Anne Rice a "friend", as I don't really know her personally, she and I have emailed a couple of times over the years and she has given me some direction both in the realms of writing, but also in publication. I follow her page and watch what she is posting. I watch how she interacts with her followers, and gain some insight from an extraordinarily successful A-lister.

Jeremy and I stay in touch pretty regularly.

I do believe the tour bought us closer together, and he is a friend.

We discuss quite a lot over the phone, much of it is writing and business related, many things are not. We are most definitely peer authors, know some things about each other's personal lives, and work on our separate projects on a similar timeline. It helps to have a "battle buddy" in this business. Someone who you can talk shop to, which is extraordinarily fun. Someone who you can tour with, and help promote, and cross promote.

A battle buddy will help you get there.

### How I will get to the next step

We're all on a journey, all of us.

Writers, artists, musicians and entrepreneurs. Our creative mediums may be different, but our mission, and our directions, are one in the same. We all seek to expand our audiences. Make sales, earn royalties or revenue, and get a whole bunch of reviews.

I know I still have a ways to go in getting to where my ultimate goals are for my writing career.

I also realize that in the years that I've logged behind me, in both a creative and a marketing perspective, I have already come a long way.

I've had numerous conversations with my close friends and family on the topics of getting to the next step. My mother said something quite profound when we would have our phone conversations and discuss my writing career. When expressing frustration about "how slow" things were progressing, she would always stop me. "Look at all the small things that have been happening," she would say. "Appreciate those small steps. They keep you going. And keep you focused."

When looking back, I understand what she meant by that.

To help support my artistic career, I also have worked as a bartender. As I had mentioned in previous chapters, while I was a manager in the hospitality business for years, I made the decision to follow my dream.

I wanted to become a full-time novelist.

That was the point in my life when I chose to step down and tend bar.

Over the course of several years, I had some discouraging thoughts when I believed I had made the wrong decision. My writing career wasn't taking off like I'd hoped. I was working full time, running around behind a bar, and I never felt that I was afforded enough creative time to get my books written. My career, in my mind, hadn't gotten to the next level on the timeline which I had initially envisioned.

However, when I looked back, I saw how much I have accomplished over the years, despite working full-time. And it's true that an extraordinary amount of creatives hold down full-time practical careers as well.

It's a lot.

We don't take days off; but we hold so much passion for our journey that the creative days become our fuel. I've been told over the years to not quit the day job too soon: that day job, however mundane it may be, becomes a creative's, or an entrepreneur's, bread and butter. The bartending allowed me to continue to create and follow my journey. It allowed me to continue to dream, but to remain being a doer while actively achieving goals.

But what my mother said caused me to pause and reflect.

One evening at the bar, a customer approached and ordered a cocktail. Pretty standard stuff.

As a bartender, I would make light conversation and the topic got around to reading and books. I mentioned to her that I was a writer, and her face lit up. "Oh! I love to read!" she exclaimed. "What's your pen name?"

"It's A.L. Mengel," I said.

And her eyes widened and her mouth dropped open. "You're kidding me. *You* are A.L. Mengel?"

I nodded.

"I have read every one of your books!"

I was floored.

That chance encounter was just the encouragement that I needed at that point in my writing career. And my mother knew it.

I'd dreamed for years of meeting a reader in a situation like that, and I was lucky enough to have it happen. Meeting that reader gave me the encouragement that I needed.

I promptly ran out to my car and fished a copy of *The Wandering Star* out of a box from the back seat, brought it back to the bar and signed it for her.

My mother, however, was right.

It's those little moments in our creative journeys that provide the precise amount of encouragement that we need to press on, and continue.

### *If all fails, I must keep trying.*

This is a tough business to break into, that's for sure. Honestly, any creative or start-up venture is a challenge. Whether it be for books, art, music, or starting a new business.

It's been a long road in this book to get to this last section.

Our journeys are similar.

There is a lengthy path before us, filled with countless stepping stones, stretching out towards the horizon. Sometimes, it will be challenging to get from one stone to the next. It might take longer than we anticipate; perhaps the stones were placed far apart.

Or perhaps we might slip on a stone.

But we will always catch our balance.

We will keep our eyes towards the horizon; looking at each stone reaching outwards, until they became too small to see.

The stones right in front of us, however, are large and supportive.

They will feel solid, like a foundation. And they will carry us towards the next stepping stone, in time.

Sometimes we will hit the next stone precisely.

There would be other times when we might make a leap over several stones at once, gradually, and methodically, getting closer towards the horizon, as the distant stones slowly approach our view.

So close, yet still so far away.

Now, fellow writer, artist, musician, entrepreneur, it's time to consider your marketing journey.

This book has offered a glimpse into my own, and I truly hope that these principles, The Four "I" Statements and The Four "How" Statements can help you on your own journey.

This methodology has certainly helped me.

The principles have helped me grow the reach on my Facebook page to nearly a half million. But as you can see, it took time.

It takes time moving forward.

I know that I still have quite a bit of stepping stones on the journey yet to discover.

# THE END

July 7, 2020 3:58pm

*Do you think you are a Wanderer…or a Crypt Dancer?*

*Enter #TheWritingStudio Now and explore your creative and artistic identity!*

*Discover your passions through art, music, philosophy and trending topics by watching introspective videos and reading speculative fiction.*

*www.facebook.com/authoralmengel*

**PUBLISHED BY PARCHMAN'S PRESS, LLC**